Mutual Respect
The Art and Practice of Quid Pro Quo Selling

HINTHORN

Copyright © 2005 Gregg Hinthorn Inc.
Published by Hinthorn Media

This publication is designed to provide accurate and authoritative information in regard to the subject matter covered. It is presented with the understanding that the publisher is not engaged in rendering legal, accounting or other professional services. If legal advice or other expert assistance is required, the services of a competent professional person should be sought.

Library of Congress Cataloging in Publication Data:
ISBN 0-9679449-6-1

Printed in the United States of America

10 9 8 7 6 5 4 3 2 1

Table of Contents

I wanted to express my great satisfaction with the impact Quid Pro Quo selling had on my sales team. Prior to meeting with you, we had invested heavily in traditional sales training that provided a formula or process that promised to lead to revenue generation, but we got little return on our investment. The last thing our sales and account executives—all seasoned veterans—wanted was more time wasted in yet "another" sales training class. By noon of the first day, however, they couldn't stop talking about Quid Pro Quo.

The sales and account team were able to put Quid Pro Quo to work immediately following the workshop. In fact, while we were still in the class, you helped one team make a quantum leap in a huge deal where we'd been struggling for months to make significant headway.

Quid Pro Quo selling was direct, hands on training that overlays the sales process our company had adopted and gave the sales force the real world tools they needed to make it work and give us the results we want.

Amy Phelps, Vice President of Sales Operations

SAP Public Services

Your Quid Pro Quo selling approach was not just another sales training class! Within five days of completing the course, my team saved two opportunities by taking control of the client situation which turned into $200,000 of closed business inside 30 days.

With Quid Pro Quo we were learning a proven approach and the techniques to put it into practice today. We look forward to continuing to work with Sales Builders, improving skills and closing more opportunities.

Robert Lasher, CEO

iPartners

There were nothing but upbeat comments on the Quid Pro Quo selling approach and training. We have had other sales training courses, but your real life, practical, and tactical approach will net us the results we need.

Lawson Y. Glenn, Director

Global Alliances

Our primary goals for sales training was to get a stable, repeatable process in place, as well as to bring about permanent behavior changes in our sales organization. To date, your QPQ selling approach has enabled us to accomplish both goals.

We have achieved our quarterly profitability goals for 12 quarters in a row. Using Sales Builders' "Franchise Mentality" approach has enabled us to achieve a +5 to -10% forecasting accuracy. In addition, our average deal size is up 44% over the same period last year and new account growth is up 90% over the same time period. We have achieved all these results with a 60% forced turnover of the sales force! I personally, along with the rest of our team, attribute much of our success this year to our use of Sales Builders' approaches.

Rick Marquardt, President
Ross Systems

I was exceptionally pleased at what I saw in your Quid Pro Quo selling approach. Your course has opened my eyes to many new practical ways to grow our revenues and has made a big difference in the way I manage and interact with my team.

Bob Neely, Vice-President of Sales
Syntex

Acknowledgements

For several years, I was President of Cray Systems. When two of the previous companies I had helped build went public the same year, I decided to resign from Cray. When I left, one of my long-time employees and dearest friends called to ask me what I was going to do next. When I told him I planned to work on my golf game, he almost jumped through the phone. He was adamant that I start a new company and help salespeople everywhere by sharing my innovative approach to selling.

That dear friend's name is Jeff Culverhouse. Without Jeff's encouragement and support, there would be no Sales Builders, Inc., Quid Pro Quo Selling, Executive Link or this book. A very heart-felt thank-you goes out to Jeff for his ongoing support and advice.

I also want to thank the clients of Sales Builders who are using the Quid Pro Quo approach. We receive emails on a regular basis from sales people who have applied my techniques and have gotten tremendous results. It's their favorable responses that makes what we do so rewarding.

I'd like to acknowledge all of the Sales Builders partners. They are each vital in helping our business grow. I'd especially like to mention Todd Madderra, from the Madderra Group, who helped put together our Executive Link product and the outstanding Sales Builders web site.

Kristen Patterson is always there to help develop anything from training materials to Executive Link content.

Gregg Hinthorn from Hinthorn Media was instrumental in publishing and distributing this book. Gregg's ideas, input and enthusiasm made this project fun and productive.

Thanks also go out to Sales Builders' world-class advisory board and partners, who always keep me between the lines and offer more help than they know: Rick Marquardt, Gene Hindman, Bob Lasher, Charlie Paparelli, and Wayne Cape.

Also the Sales Builders employees deserve thanks. They are in the field every day, spreading the good word about the Quid Pro Quo sales approach. Special thanks go to our first two employees Dick Ransom and Betsy Cagle.

Thank you to Ralph and Corrine Walker for offering their unwavering support to family and me. Without them, this book may never have been completed.

I want to thank the two people who got this whole thing started. George Beck is always there to offer insight on any subject at any time. Dee Beck has always been my biggest cheerleader, offering nothing but encouragement for everything I do.

Even though this book is dedicated to my wife and children, it would be a mistake not to thank the other family members and friends who inspire me everyday in everything I do. They make it all worthwhile, and, without their love and support, none of this would be possible.

Dedications

This book is dedicated to my family who offers me unconditional love and support. I am inspired daily by my wife Laurie, sons Robbie, Tyler, Nick and daughter Melissa.

This book is also dedicated to sales people who have not yet seen the results they desire. You were all the inspiration for *Mutual Respect*.

Foreword

I first met Bob Beck when we both worked for Computron Technologies. Bob was the VP of Sales; I was learning how to be a pre-sales consultant. As part of my training, I attended one of Bob's classes. Everyone else in the class was a veteran, and I was obviously the new kid. Bob's topic was "The 10 Attributes of Top Sales Consultants." I had a million questions, and judging from the looks of the others in the class, most of my questions were about things they already knew.

I was impressed with Bob's enthusiasm and the fact that he treated me, the new guy, with respect. He wanted to make sure I understood every facet of what he had to say. It was absolutely clear that he wanted me to be successful.

It turned out that I was.

And after I learned Bob's system, I was also pretty confident I could succeed in my own business. I left Computron and started Systems Conversion, Ltd., a consulting and programming firm that works exclusively with interBiz™ Supply Chain Group's PRMS™ software. Fortunately, Bob agreed to be both my mentor and consultant.

We started out as a two-person operation and have subsequently grown to more than 45 employees. Over five years (through 2000) our sales increased more than 1,000%. Our clients include Akzo Nobel, Robert Bosch, Godiva Chocolates and Owens Corning. As a result, we've been named to the *Inc.* 500 as one of the fastest-growing, privately-owned businesses in America.

Does the Quid Pro Quo selling method work?

Absolutely.

Is it a good investment?

Without doubt.

You want more proof? Every month I pay for Bob to visit our company. We review our progress against where we want to be, and we make any necessary changes based on new competition, the state of the economy and other factors. Every penny I invest in the Quid Pro Quo selling approach comes back a hundredfold. Bob's program gives us the tools we need to come out on top.

Jeff Culverhouse, President and CEO

Systems Conversion, Ltd.

April, 2004

Introduction

"The world we live in has changed. The way business is done has changed, too. What have you changed about your sales approach to meet these new challenges?"

Like many young people in college, I had no idea what I wanted to do for a living. After every year of college, my mother would tell me, "Don't worry, son, you will know what you want to do." By the time I was a senior at the University of Cincinnati, I doubted whether or not I'd ever know what I wanted to do. I knew I wanted to make a lot of money and control my own destiny, but I had no clue how to do this.

While home from school on vacation, I received some direction from my mother that set the stage for a long and rewarding sales career. She had met a twenty-four-year-old young man who worked for a computer company and made $125,000 per year. (To put things into perspective, at that time the average income for college grads was $14,000 per year.) His income sounded like a fortune! I found out the name of the company and called three times a day for fourteen days. Finally, they hired me.

I flew to California, and the company picked me up from the airport in a limo. On the ride to the office, it suddenly hit me that I knew absolutely nothing about computers, had very little sales experience, and would probably be on the next plane home as soon as they figured this out. Through extreme fear, uncertainty, and doubt, as well as the basic need to survive, I developed the principles of the Quid Pro Quo sales approach you are about to learn. These principles have changed my life, and I sincerely hope they will change yours as well.

Why Did I Write This Book?

I have yet to hear of a major university or college that offers a B.A. in sales. Since so many of us make our living in sales, it seems like it would be one of the most popular majors available. According to research, 94% of all salespeople have had fewer than five days of formal sales training. Ninety percent of sales managers have had fewer than eight days of formal sales training.

The salespeople or companies who do invest in sales courses find most training falls short of actually providing tools that can be applied in the real world. Sales representative do not need the theory of selling; they need an actual process they can use to close business. Also, the world we live in has changed. The way business is done has changed. Yet most sales people have not changed their sales approach. Hopefully this book will help you make the needed changes to your approach.

Product Training is Not Sales Training

Because there is very little reality-oriented training for professional selling, it's no wonder so many representatives struggle to meet expectations. Companies spend days and days and have an unlimited budget for product training but often overlook sales training entirely. Success is sales-driven, not product-driven. For example, where are all the dot-coms that had great products but could not sell them successfully?

Unfortunately, many fast-growing start-ups and some larger organizations think their products are so good they will sell themselves. They think that if their sales people know enough about the product, then surely they will be successful. But there is far more to selling than product knowledge.

Remember, this is not your father's sales approach! With all the changes going on in business, you must adopt a new sales approach to maximize your results. You must change your perspectives and have courage. You must develop a different action plan to realize the consistent results you want. Quid Pro Quo selling should inspire you to make significant changes in your selling style. Merely reading this book is easy. Becoming disciplined enough to adopt and follow the principles of Quid Pro Quo selling on a daily basis may challenge you. You must make a commitment to the program and stick with it.

It takes three weeks to form a habit. A habit can turn into a discipline. If you discipline yourself on a daily basis, eventually something magical will happen, almost without you realizing it. One day, the discipline turns into desire.

So, right now, today, start changing your results by adopting the principles of this book. If you work through a little pain, I promise you'll see a little progress, then more progress, then significant progress.

SECTION ONE

The Foundation of Mutual Respect

CHAPTER ONE

You Can Be Successful

Everybody sells. Every day. Whether you realize it or not, whether you're professional or not, or whether you're any good at it or not, you sell. I sell. The person next door sells. Here are some examples.

You and your spouse decide to go out for dinner. You want Chinese. Your spouse wants Italian. How do you decide where to go? Does one of you sell the other on your choice? You bet. Is it a give-and-take process? Of course. This is the classic process of selling—one person persuading another to take his route to improvement, success or pleasure.

You go to the bank to apply for a loan. In the process, you give the loan officer a sales pitch to sell him on the idea that you are a good risk.

You apply for a job, selling the potential employer on the belief that you're the person the company needs to hire. You're selling yourself.

Some of the best natural salespeople are children. I have four of them, so I have much experience in this area. When I ask one of my children to do a chore, this child tries instantly to sell me on the idea of why the smallest task can't be done. "I don't know how." "I'm too little." As a parent, my job is to convince the child that the task is manageable and that there is a good reason for him or her to do it.

The point is, everybody sells. Every day.

Mutual Respect, however, was written to help people whose careers are in sales. Each day, thousands of men and women step out into the world representing themselves, their companies, and their products or the services they provide. Each salesperson tries to identify prospects and show them why his company's particular product or service will enhance their businesses or personal lives. Ultimately, he wants each of these prospects to buy the product or service. Each salesperson acts according to the classic definition of selling: creating demand, winning acceptance, and transferring money from buyer to seller.

The Quid Pro Quo sales approach offers a well-defined, systematic and repeatable process that can raise your sales success to a new level. By applying this approach and using aggressive, professional and creative sales skills, you'll enjoy sales success that far exceeds your expectations.

Mutual Respect addresses specific areas of sales to help give you the tools which will serve you throughout your sales career. It also gives you many practical examples of how using the Quid Pro Quo selling approach will give you a repeatable and predictable process.

What is Quid Pro Quo Selling?

Quid pro quo is a Latin term which means "what for what." Something is given in exchange for something else. Common usage has modified this definition to mean an equal exchange or substitution. Something of value is given in exchange for something else of value. When it comes to selling, the essence of quid pro quo is money given in exchange for a desired product or service.

Many other kinds of exchanges, however, will occur throughout your sales cycle. For instance, a prospect asks you to send her more information about your product. What do you do in response? Mail the prospect your slick pocket folder stuffed with information in hope that she will read all of your marketing materials and be ready to buy on the very next phone call? That is not selling. That is hoping. Producing, writing, printing and mailing those materials cost money.

What happens in such an approach? You must make multiple phone calls to get back in contact with the prospect. Then after several days or weeks pass you finally get your prospect on the phone and she says, "Oh, yes, Bob, thanks for sending me the literature. I haven't gotten around to looking at it yet, but I will real soon."

You say, "Okay," and hang up. That's reacting, not selling, you have lost control of the sales cycle.

Would your attitude change about sending out marketing materials if you were charged a fee for each one you sent out? In one of the Quid Pro Quo training classes, I told the group they would be charged for everything: brochures, company resources, and travel. They believed me. When I told them I was kidding and then asked if they would change their day-to-day actions if that were their plan, they responded, "Yes!" That was the wrong answer, but it was the honest one.

Quid Pro Quo calls for sending materials the prospect requested but also getting something back. What would you like in return that would help move your sales cycle along and help you stay in control? You want the prospect to read the materials and be prepared to talk to you about the products at a set time. So, next time you're asked to send your marketing literature, say, "Mr. Prospect, I'd be happy to send our literature for your review. When would be a good day and time for us to discuss the materials?"

This method keeps you in control and your sales cycle moving forward. If the prospect can't give you a date and time, don't waste your materials hoping he might actually review the literature and buy from you. Hundreds of reasonable exchanges like this are part of the sales cycle.

However, Quid Pro Quo is more than a single currency-for-goods transaction. It's a proven, career-building approach. It enables you to identify qualified prospects, create respectful relationships with them, and control all of the aspects of the sales process.

The era when representatives allow prospects to control the selling process is long gone. If you're going to be successful, the relationship you create with your prospect must be a continual series of compromises by both parties. These compromises begin with the first contact and don't end until the agreement is signed. If you are unable to establish this type of relationship, a Quid Pro Quo relationship, then you don't have a prospect worthy of your effort. Life is too short and your time is too valuable, so move on to a prospect who is interested in solving her issues, not one who wants to play a sales game.

An exercise: Write down all the things prospects ask you for in the course of a sales cycle. Consider what you'd like in return. Write down these ideas, and then try them in your next sales call.

If you struggle with this, try remembering that the three main things you want in return are:

1. Access
2. Information
3. Partnership

Think of past sales cycles where you had unlimited access to the decision-makers. What did they want? What did you want from them? Look at the following chart and write down the responses you'd like to see from a prospect.

Typical Request From Prospects

Meeting

RFP/RFQ

Pricing

Meet Management

Proposal

References

Site Visit

Presentation

Figure 1.1

Most people do not have much trouble filling in the above exercise. However, to be a real Quid Pro Quo master, you also will have to sell the prospect on why his effort in the sales relationship will benefit him. This give-and-take is challenging and invaluable.

The Quid Pro Response to a Typical Request

Meeting	Decision makers to attend
RFP/RFQ	Understanding of preconceived notions
Pricing	Timeline for decision/budget
Meet Management	Meet their management
Proposal	Present in person
References	Agree on price and terms
Site Visit	Agree on price and terms
Presentation	All economic decision makers present

Figure 1.2

The key to the Quid Pro Quo exchange is selling the prospect on why it is good for them as seen in figure 1.3

This exercise becomes a bit more challenging in Figure 1.2. It may not come naturally, so work at it a bit or attend one of our Sales Builders Quid Pro Quo courses (see www.salesbuilders.com) until this method becomes second nature.

Training, Experience and Determination

Selling is like sailing a boat. Generally, you need some instruction to be able to sail. After a few lessons, most people can guide their boats from one point to another, but the trouble comes when they have to turn back. My father, whose passion is sailing, has figured this out, but he is not ready to sail a boat in an America's Cup race. At that top level, you need expert training, experience and determination.

The same is true if you want to be a top professional salesperson. Many sales people can succeed because they're at the right place at the right time or the economy is really booming or the marketing department has them inundated with leads, but what happens when the economy is challenging or when they are not selling the hottest product on the market?

The answer is in becoming an expert, a top sales professional, who takes responsibility for his or her own success and utilizes the Quid Pro Quo approach.

CASE STUDY

New Car Salesman

One of the many jobs I had while working my way through college was selling cars. I took the job for two reasons: first, I was a starving, poverty-stricken college student; and second, every career job in the paper required a college degree and sales experience, and I had met neither of those qualifications.

Thus, I went to work part-time selling Lincoln Continentals and Town Cars. These things were boats on wheels. At the time, gas prices were the highest in my life. Getting just 8 miles per gallon, these cars were true gas-guzzlers. So why would anyone buy one when there were other cars on the market that got better mileage and would actually fit into a standard-sized garage?

When I accepted this part-time job, I committed to treating people exactly as I wanted to be treated when I looked at cars. Years later, this same commitment turned out to be one of the key ingredients in Quid Pro Quo selling. At the dealership, the veteran sales people stood around complaining about the gas prices and the price of the cars we were selling. Sure, market conditions were terrible, but they were compounded by the fact that the worst salespeople usually have the best and most creative excuses for why they can't sell.

I can't say for sure if my success was due to the fact that I was just too dumb to understand that you can't sell gas-guzzlers during a gas crisis, or if it was my belief that you have to treat people the way you would like to be treated. Maybe it was driven by my burning desire to earn some money. Whatever it was, I sold thirty cars my first month as a salesman. The next month I sold twenty-seven more. At the time, a salesman was considered to have had a good month if he sold four to five cars.

While I was at the dealership, I saw a lot of sales people come and go. Each used the same old excuses for their failures. Not one of them said he needed to improve his sales skills.

CHAPTER TWO

Why Quid Pro Quo Selling
is Necessary

Many people don't understand the role of the sales representative. Even the companies that hire sales people often think the services or products the company provides are so superior to the rest of the market that they will actually sell themselves. For this reason, sales people are often considered to be merely order takers or, at best, a necessary part of doing business.

Let me set the record straight. The function of the sales person is to get and keep new customers. Without these new customers, a company will not grow, and, frankly, if a company isn't growing and moving forward, then it's falling behind. Its chances of surviving are bleak. Sales representatives are critical to a company's success: they put the wood on the fire!

When any kind of salesperson approaches a prospective buyer, typically the buyer's automatic "Sales Security System" activates. Lights flash and alarms sound in their mind. The Sales Security System is an invisible wall that protects the prospective buyer from the sales person's clever ways to get them to buy something.

The Sales Security System is especially sensitive when you go out to buy a new car. In fact, as soon as you hit the new car lot, your Sales Security System is activated!

And why not? You wouldn't want that clever car salesmen to put you in the wrong vehicle. And besides, you're only there to look, right? You never know what magic potions or secret tricks the salesperson might use to get you to buy a car that day.

Maybe not. In truth, this entire Sales Security System process is a little ridiculous, but that's how virtually every buyer is programmed. In sales, you need to learn how to turn off that security system. Understanding the psychological basis behind each prospect's Sales Security System is one of the fundamental parts of Quid Pro Quo Selling.

Assume that you are back at the car lot and a salesman approaches. In a low-key way, he introduces himself, finds out your needs and desires for a car, and then asks you how he can serve you best. Let's further assume that you answer the question, "How can I serve you?" with a clever comeback, such as, "I'm just looking."

To your surprise, the salesman's response is, "Great. Please take your time. Make yourself at home. I'm available to answer any questions that you may have." Doesn't your anxiety come down some? You suddenly become more relaxed and feel better about your sales person. You've just turned your security system down a notch.

Selling vs. Giving a Prospect the Opportunity to Buy

I can honestly say I've never sold anything in my life. On the other hand, I've given people the opportunity to buy millions and millions of dollars worth of the products I have represented. There's a big difference, and this difference is part of the foundation for Quid Pro Quo selling. You must be aware of the prospect's Sales Security System as you approach each opportunity.

EXERCISE: WRITE DOWN ALL THE PHRASES THAT MIGHT TURN

ON THE SALES SECURITY SYSTEM.

"I'VE GOT A DEAL FOR YOU."

"THE PRICE IS GOING UP."

"WE ONLY HAVE A FEW LEFT."

Perception is Reality

In sales, the way that you, your company and your company's solution are perceived means everything. In my experience, the perception is generally far more important than the reality. Virtually all successful sales people realize that understanding how people perceive you is one of the keys to sales success. In sales, the statement that perception is reality is true.

Since being perceived as a salesperson activates the prospect's Sales Security System, let's consider what specifically triggers the alarm. Here are some reasons why you might be perceived as a sales quota person:

1. Prospects don't trust you.
2. Prospects assume that, since you are on commission, all you care about is making a sale.
3. Prospects assume you don't care about their needs and issues.
4. Prospects assume you don't listen.
5. Prospects assume you're trying to take advantage of them.

In order to overcome these negative assumptions and stereotypes, you should be perceived as a business consultant and as a doctor—a sales doctor, so to speak. You want to be a "Trusted Advisor."

Are you a Trusted Advisor?

Think about the times you have purchased expensive items. Don't you feel more comfortable when the salesperson asks you questions that demonstrates that she is really trying to understand your needs? The sense of bonding that comes when problems are solved jointly is the basis for creating a successful sales relationship. Combining good questions with sympathetic listening and then offering solid advice makes you an expert and trusted adviser.

1. How are executives judged?
2. What keeps them awake at night?
3. What are their hot buttons?
4. What are the top 10 things this role has issues with?
5. Why does this role get promoted or fired?
6. Who else in the organization is affected by their performance?
7. Can your team discuss the latest industry trends?
8. Is your team comfortable standing toe to toe with executives

Prospect Request	Response	Why It's Good for Prospects
Meeting	Decision makers to attend.	They won't have to attend multiple meetings.
RFP/RFQ	Understanding of preconceived notions.	The more information they send, the more complete solutions you'll be able to provide.
Pricing	Timeline for decision/budget.	You'll be able to offer them the best price and answer questions immediately by being in person.
Meet Management	Meet management.	Get all players involved to share any perceived risk.
Proposal	Present in person.	
References	Agree on price and terms.	
Site Visit	Agree on price and terms.	
Presentation	All economic decision makers present.	

FIGURE 1.3

creating a QPQ relationship?

9. Can your team build value for your solution at the executive level?

10. How often do they start their selling efforts at the executive level?

11. Do they have overwhelming credibility early in the sales cycle?

Many organizations talk about employing a "consultative sales" approach. This is the foundation of the Quid Pro Quo sales approach. During our training workshops, we ask sales people what a consultative sales approach means to them. Most people understand the concept but don't know how to employ the consultative approach to selling.

If you start your cold calls with, "Hi, Mr. Prospect. My name is Bob Beck from ABC Company. How are you today?" You will quickly activate your prospect's inner Sales Security System. If your prospect's next thought is, "What is he selling?" then you are not using a consultative sales approach.

Most business consultants are hired to help an organization identify and resolve issues they may be facing. When I'm in this role, I'm hired for my past experience, track record, reputation and expertise. My sole objective is to help the company who has hired me. There is no hidden agenda, no politics and no other reason for me to be there. Let's look at the attributes of a business consultant.

- Helps
- Listens
- Advises
- Guides
- Makes recommendations
- Corrects misconceptions
- Is an expert
- Has conviction
- Has credibility

These attributes are exactly what your prospect is looking for in a good consultative sales person. The best consultants not only are perceived as having the attributes noted above but also actually have them.

You need to have the conviction that your product is indeed serving your prospects' best interest. If this is the case, this conviction will come across in all your discussions. If you don't believe in your product, then you need to find one you can believe in.

The other way a sales person might want to be perceived is as a sales doctor. Time after time, I've started a sales call and specifically told prospects to think of me as a doctor. I tell them the better they can describe the pain, problem or issues, the better job I can do to prescribe a solution. Then I sit back and listen.

The relationship is often similar to that which takes place between Tony and his therapist on "The Sopranos." The therapist does almost no talking and all the listening. She asks Tony a few questions, then sits back and waits for the responses. My favorite questions of hers are: "Why do you think it's like this? How long has it been this way? What do you think the cure is?" In the end, he gives her all the answers.

This is exactly the way it should be in a positive exchange between a sales person and a prospect. You should be the doctor, asking open-ended questions, getting the prospect to relax and tell you her issues. Be sincerely interested in your prospect's financial health and prescribe beneficial solutions, and you'll be perceived as a sales doctor, a trusted adviser.

All prospects think their particular situations are unique, but in actuality, the situations that companies face are often similar. As a good doctor, you'll want to let each prospect share his pain completely. Why? Because the more distinct he thinks his problems are, the more distinct they will perceive your solution to be.

Let's Play Poker

Some of you like to gamble more than others. Most of us would not want to gamble our family or personal futures away, though. After you read this book, I'd like to play poker with whomever would like to play. I get to make the rules, and I'll let you know if you win or lose.

Nobody in their right mind would play a poker game where the rules are set or changed and you find out if you won or lost after every hand. What is really bad is if winning a pot or two keeps you playing in the game.

Doesn't this happen to us more times than we want to admit when we are selling? The prospect is in total control. They set the rules of the evaluation and we find out at the end of the sales cycle if we won or lost. It is not much different then a rigged poker game. You need to establish a Quid Pro Quo relationship to understand the prospect's expectations. You want to know you at least have an even playing field. If you don't apply the Quid Pro Quo approach, then you are really just gambling with your career, your earnings and your future.

CHAPTER THREE

The Rules of Quid Pro Quo Selling

To be effective in sales, you have to establish a relationship. The relationships that succeed are the ones that have an established give-and-take to them. Something is exchanged for something else. Quid Pro Quo.

Selling is no different. The first rule in Quid Pro Quo selling is to establish a give-and-take relationship with your prospects. Never give anything away unless you get something back.

Very few salespeople feel empowered to set the guidelines for a give-and-take relationship with their prospects. Quid Pro Quo selling is all about creating and keeping this type of relationship throughout the sales cycle. If you want to be perceived as a business consultant instead of merely a salesperson, it's critical that you establish give-and-take guidelines with your prospects. Always keep in mind you're trying to help your prospects solve problems and meet their needs.

The most effective approach to establishing a give-and-take relationship for each sales opportunity is to approach it as if you were selling to yourself. If you act in a way that would turn on your own Sales Security System, then you can be pretty sure your actions will turn on that of your prospects.

The second rule in Quid Pro Quo selling is to always put yourself in your prospect's shoes. Think about the method you currently use when you approach your prospects. Would you buy from you? If you answered, "No" or "Not all the time," then you need to change your approach. By putting your own personality into the relationship and genuinely looking out for the best interests of the buyer, you'll naturally have more sincerity, conviction and comfort throughout the sales cycle.

A successful sales relationship is built on the same kind of trust on which friendships and even marriages are built. You need to empathize with the wants, needs, interests and motives of the other person in the relationship. Take the time to find out enough about a person so that you can empathize with her. In return, let her learn something about you. Such knowledge enables you to establish that essential give-and-take relationship. You're not adversaries, but teammates working toward the same goal.

Dealing with your prospects on a personal level makes the job a lot more enjoyable. Business doesn't have to be, and shouldn't be, all about business. When it's all business, everyone becomes inflexible and stuffy. The Sales Security System activates, and the entire experience becomes much more tedious. Even the most unlikable people you come across most likely will have some interest or characteristic that you can admire. Almost all prospects deserve your sincere interest.

It's your responsibility as a sales representative to find some common ground with your prospects and to let them know you care about them as people. This honest concern will set you apart from other vendors who come along, give a canned sales pitch and leave.

The best way to find out this information is to ask open-ended questions. For example, when you are given a referral, ask the person giving you the name to tell you about the person being referred. This bit of information can get a prospect talking and move you on your way to building rapport.

....

QUESTIONS FOR BUILDING RAPPORT:

WHERE DID YOU GROW UP?

WHAT COLLEGE DID YOU ATTEND?

DO YOU HAVE ANY KIDS?

WHAT IS YOUR JOB HISTORY?

WHAT ARE YOUR FAVORITE HOBBIES?

WHAT ARE YOUR BUSINESS GOALS?

WHAT ARE YOUR FAVORITE SPORTS TEAMS?

Practically anything at all can work. Asking good questions can win or lose a sale. All sales people should perfect this step.

CASE STUDY

Bonding Bob

Many years ago, I began calling on Lakeland Regional Medical Center, selling mainframe application software for M.S.A (Management Sciences of America). My nickname at M.S.A. was "Bonding Bob" because I spent a lot of time trying to get know my prospects on a personal level.

The CIO of the hospital was an elderly gentleman, experienced and extremely tough. He was one of those guys who says, "Okay, I've got fifteen minutes. What do you have?" He'd been a VP of sales, president of a company, and CIO, so he had seen it all. It took me two lunches and another separate sales call to get him to even show me a crack in the door. But, since he represented a $750,000 opportunity, and since he was definitely going to buy from either my competitor or me, I felt it worth a few calls to try to open him up a bit.

At our second lunch, he told me he had moved to Florida from the Northeast because his wife suffered from severe asthma. Even though the hospital was in Lakeland, they lived in Sarasota because they both loved sailing. That was all I needed to hear. The timing was perfect. Without missing a beat, I told him my wife and I were planning to go sailing. "Since we'll both be in Sarasota," I said, "would you and your wife like to join us?" He gladly accepted and said he looked forward to it.

Now all I had to do was find a forty-one-foot sailboat and a captain, identify a weekend that my wife and I could be in Sarasota and get my manager to approve the expenses for this excursion! I knew if I could get the CIO and his wife out on the boat for the afternoon, my chances of winning his business would increase dramatically. Mutual respect is built on knowledge and trust, and a relaxed social setting can quickly facilitate the process of getting to know one another.

I organized the outing, and the CIO and his wife showed up as scheduled. We sailed for three hours. Everyone got along great and exchanged lots of personal information.

We lunched together after docking, which only enhanced the experience. When we finished, the prospect's wife kissed me and told me I reminded her of her son! From that point on, my relationship with the hospital's CIO was bonded for good. The sale was pretty much closed as soon as we got off that boat.

The third rule of Quid Pro Quo Selling is that the prospect is not always right. Too many sales people believe they have to provide customers with whatever they want, whenever they want. The common wisdom is that they have to give in or they will have no chance to sell. They assume that saying "No" will alienate their prospects and drive them to buy from competitors. Whoever bends over fastest and farthest wins the business, right?

Wrong! You are in the selling business, not the service business. Waiters, flight attendants, and bartenders provide service. You are selling!

It's important that you understand where the line is. The foundation of the Quid Pro Quo sales approach is about forming an equal relationship between buyer and seller. Think about any successful relationship in your life. How many times would you call your neighbors and take them to dinner without any reciprocation? How many times would you call someone for a date with no return phone call? Human nature says you won't do that very long. Why would you want to continue a one-way relationship with a buyer?

Think about the dynamics in most buyer and seller relationships. Too many times, sales people fall into the habit of acting as if they are the buyer's trick dog, jumping through hoop after hoop, hoping to please. Quid Pro Quo is about selling as a subject expert in a true consultative sales approach. It's about establishing an equal give-and-take relationship with the buyer.

Sales people are encumbered by the notion, "People buy from people they like." Maybe this is true, but it also is true that people buy from people they respect.

Let's test this statement. Let's say you shop at a couple of electronics stores for a new sound system. At the first store, the sales person is pierced, tattooed, has long, greasy hair and hasn't shaved in three days. He is an expert on sound systems, however, and understands your needs and gives you great advice. At the next store the salesman is clean-cut, but he has to keep pulling out the marketing materials to look up the answers to your questions. The point is, you might not want to have a beer with the tattooed sales person, but you will respect his expertise and be more likely to buy from him than from the clean-cut guy.

CASE STUDY

Southwest Portland Cement

This case study demonstrates a key principle of the Quid Pro Quo sales approach: You must set boundaries. Note the things I would and wouldn't do to win business.

I was a senior executive for a small but growing self-funded software company based in Hyannis, Massachusetts. One day a company representative asked me to accompany him on a trip to Houston, Texas, to visit Southwest Portland Cement Company. This company wanted a short presentation of our financial application software followed by a question-and-answer session with thirty of their controllers. The representative had done a good job with qualification, and we felt Southwest Portland Cement was a worthy prospect.

When we showed up, the room was filled with accountants and controllers, as well as Larry, the decision maker and company's Chief Informational Officer (CIO). We gave our presentation, and things went well.

Larry, whom we'd discovered had a huge ego, decided he had to show me his computer room, something I personally had no interest in seeing. When we got there, I listened to him discuss at length the different pieces of computer hardware, the configurations and the special flooring he'd installed.

While bragging about his hardware, Larry also let me know exactly what he expected from us. He told me that Southwest Portland Cement was an IBM showcase account and that many people would be touring the company to see the latest technologies available. This could ultimately mean a lot of business for our company. Because of this, he expected a 50% discount, free software customizations, a full-time person on site to help them implement the solution, and other things.

I listened, knowing that we weren't going to be able to give him anything on his long list of requests. Whenever I tried to explain why we couldn't accommodate him, he just talked over me and reminded me about Southwest Portland Cement's being an IBM showcase account.

When I returned to headquarters, I called the sales person and told him about my conversation with the CIO. I told him not to waste his time on this account because, even if we could meet Larry's expectations, there was no way he would pay our price or accept our terms. A few days later, I received a call from the CIO saying he needed a technical review of our product in Houston in four days. I informed him that we did not give technical reviews and we would not be coming to Houston. The CIO became very indignant and quickly let me know our competition was happy to accommodate him. I apologized and said we'd have to pass.

A few days later, the CIO called again. He wanted to know if he could bring his team to Hyannis to take an in-depth look at our product. Since he was willing to fly six people across the country to see our product, and since I was already in Hyannis, I readily agreed.

After the usual greetings, we walked into the sales meeting. The president and founder of my company decided to sit in, something he rarely did. Since I didn't expect him to attend, I had not prepped him on my conversation with the CIO back in Houston.

The CIO sat at the head of the big conference table, and my president sat at the other end. To start the meeting, Larry sat back and said, "Bob, I apologize for not talking to you about this first, but..."—and here he turned to my company's founder—"Mr. President, we almost didn't come up here today. Getting anything out of your sales force has been like pulling teeth. We don't think you want our business very badly, and we don't appreciate the treatment we've received throughout our evaluation." If looks could kill, the one I got from the president of my company would have put me six feet under.

I asked if I could address the CIO's comments. "Larry, you told me in Houston that you are an IBM showcase account, that you wanted a 50% discount, several free modifications to the software, a person to stay on site until you are fully implemented, and more. Is that correct?"

He leaned back in his chair with a smirk on his face, and said, "Absolutely."

With that I stood up, put my hand out, and said, "Let's end this meeting right now so you guys can enjoy a nice day on the Cape." As if we had rehearsed it, the president of my company stood up also and extended his hand as well.

Larry looked confused and was quite flustered. I reminded him again of his wish list and expectations. Then I let him know that searching for freebies wasn't a prudent way to evaluate software. Furthermore, since we weren't going to meet any of his expectations, why waste any more time? I looked him right in the eye and said, "Now, if you were going to evaluate the software based on the strength of our company, our technology and our ability to meet your business requirements, I know we would earn your business, but that's not what you're telling us."

Larry quickly recanted, sat down and affirmed that the things I had just mentioned were his criteria as well. His additional requests were just nice things to have. In all honesty, I really got a lot of satisfaction out of Larry's backtracking!

Ultimately, Southwest Portland Cement paid list price for our software. We didn't give them a single item on their wish list, and, believe it or not, Larry ended up being one of our best references.

This story illustrates many of the underlying principles of Quid Pro Quo selling. A respectful give-and-take relationship throughout the sales cycle combined with some direct, bold qualifications simply made the difference.

SECTION TWO
The Way of Mutual Respect

CHAPTER FOUR

Business and Personal Planning

In order to succeed in Quid Pro Quo selling (and in life), you need to have a plan. Almost every business has a general, often philosophical, plan which provides the foundation for which more specific decisions are made. For most companies, this general plan is expressed as a mission statement.

The mission statement for Sales Builders, Inc.:

The mission of Sales Builders, Inc., is to partner with emerging organizations to ensure they realize their full potential. Our goal is to partner with each of our clients to develop, implement and execute customized business strategies for success. As part of this process, we provide professional development programs that focus on results and measures the success of our joint efforts.

Many times throughout my sales career, knowing and integrating a company's mission into my sales presentation made the difference in winning the sale. When you understand a company's mission, you know best how your product or service can meet your prospect's needs.

Business Plans

When you break down a mission statement into specific actions which must be taken within a specific time span in order to achieve specific results, then you've created a business plan. Most companies have three or five-year business plans that serve as road maps to their success.

Business plans set forth specific goals and detail the actions that must be taken in order to achieve those goals. They typically provide checkpoints along the way so that a company can monitor its progress toward its goal. For example, a retail chain might want to capture a certain percentage of its market. In order to do so, it needs to add a certain number of stores per year for a certain number of years. The business plan establishes how many stores must be added and by when.

Goals

It's human nature to see a man or a women in great shape and say, "I wish I looked liked that." Or maybe there's a very successful sales person in your company, and you say, "I wish I had her numbers." The confusion exists because the goal hasn't been broken down into achievable parts. Before you can get into great shape, for example, you've got to find a gym and develop and follow a program.

Eventually you'll get into decent shape. If you want to get into great shape, you'll need to increase your level of fitness by augmenting the program you started with. The point is, success starts with goals. Achievable goals. Goals that can be built on, so that they can carry you to your ultimate goal.

Our attitude is about the only thing we can control in our lives. If you think negatively, are filled with doubt, and are always saying, "I can't," then you won't. I guarantee it! If you have a positive attitude, however, strive toward your goal, and let nothing dilute your quest, then you stand a reasonable chance of succeeding. It all starts with your goals.

....

YOUR GOALS SHOULD BE:

BIG

LONG-TERM

SHORT-TERM

WRITTEN

SHARED

SIGNED

Personal Plans

If you want to be a successful salesperson, you'll need to have both a professional mission statement and a personal mission statement. These two mission statements are related; your professional life usually provides the means to achieve your personal mission. For example, the money you earn at work provides the security you want for your family.

Personal plans are modeled on a business-plan structure, but they are applied to both your personal and professional lives. You might want to provide security for your family. You might want to send your children to college. Or you could be working towards a comfortable retirement. Whatever your personal mission, a personal business plan helps to achieve it.

Your professional mission statement generally is more specific than your personal mission statement. You might want to hit a certain sales volume within the next year, or you might want to be promoted to district sales manager. Whatever your professional mission, you'll need, at the minimum, a one-year plan.

Personal Plans for Life Success

Here's one of Bonding Bob's great truths: When we firmly believe in what we do in our professional lives, it impacts our personal lives. This is absolutely the case with my family. Once a year each one of us makes a personal plan for life success. We follow the mission-statement and business-plan format. As each year's goals are met, we raise our expectations for the upcoming year.

How it worked for my son Rob

Rob was a good athlete growing up but not the biggest, not the fastest, and not the strongest. Football was his favorite sport. At some point, Rob decided he wanted to play Division I football at a major university. When he turned 15, I suggested we sit down and put together a written plan for the coming year to help him reach his goal. You can imagine how stupid this seemed to him as a teenager, but I convinced him to give it a shot.

Rob's goal was lofty. Here's what he was up against. Of all the young men who play football in high school, fewer than 1% move on to play at the next level. Nevertheless, we worked together to determine what qualities and measurable statistics would make his goal attainable. We came up with a written plan that included all kinds of statistics: weight lifted, forty-yard dash times, yards per carry, body weight—practically anything we could think of. We determined where these numbers needed to be when Rob was a senior and then established goals for each year. We also included academic and family goals as well.

Rob achieved his goals, I'm proud to say, through a lot of hard work and commitment to his plan. He not only received a five-year football scholarship to Rice, one of the finest universities in the nation, but also he was their starting fullback as a freshman. He led the team in scoring and was voted newcomer of the year. After his sophomore year, Rob was on track to be his school's all-time scoring leader, and he's considered one of the top running backs in his conference. Playing on Sundays after the next couple of years is within his sights.

Rob's case study shows how business methodology worked to produce life success. It's one of the great joys of parenthood to be able to share what you've learned with your children.

Personal Plans for Professional Success: Your Franchise Plan

Personal plans are essential for business success. From a sales perspective, the mission is to get and keep customers. Everything else is secondary. Unfortunately, too many salespeople race off in search of customers without a well-thought-out plan that tells them 1) how or where to find their customers and 2) what to do with them once they've found them. Your personal plan for professional success will provide the directions you need.

At the very minimum, you should consider three key questions when you create your personal business plan.

1. What's the most favorable thing that can happen to me, my family, or company this year?

2. What's the least favorable thing that could happen?

3. What can I do right now to make sure the most favorable things happen and the least favorable thing doesn't?

Once you've answered these questions, you're ready to create your professional business plan, or, as I often call it, the "Franchise Plan." Regardless of who employs you, if you are in sales, you work for yourself. This plan should list your goals for the coming year and how these goals will be achieved. You should review the plan with your manager, agree on it, and commit to it. You should also announce your plan to your colleagues, friends, and family. Why? Because once a plan is made public, you're much more likely to stick with it.

You should check your performance frequently against your plan. This will take time and discipline, but it will keep you on track. The first time someone suggested to me that I do this, I thought it would be a complete waste of my valuable time. However, after I thought through a plan, wrote it down, signed it and committed to it, surprisingly I achieved almost every aspect of the plan. Plan your work and work your plan.

Following is a detailed outline that I recommend to all the representatives who go through our training course:

Sales Representative Business Plan Outline

I. Personal Plan
    A. Personal Mission Statement
    A. Objectives
    B. Business personal improvement plan
    C. Financial
    D. Business (how much do I want to sell for the year)
    E. Current year quotas/objectives and goals
        Quota /objective
        Goals
    F. Job description/responsibilities
    G. Sales history
    H. Personal history

II. Numbers Section
    A. Percentage of goal attainment
    B. Forecast Revenue (Spreadsheet)

1. By month
2. By partner
3. By marketing activity

C. Funnel

D. Opportunities

E. Targeted accounts

F. Pipeline

III. Creative Marketing Plan

A. How are you going to get there?

B. Dates and activities

C. Expected results

D. Budget

E. Customer referrals

F. Other lead generating activities
1. Cold calling plan
2. List of connectors

IV. Ongoing Activity

A. Daily Activity Chart

B. Times spent on each activity

C. Summary by week

D. Current year forecast (spreadsheet)
1. By month
2. By product
3. By referral/business partnership

E. Expectations (by specific date)

F. Milestones

G. Achievements

Signature and date

This last part—the signatures and date—is important so everyone is on the same page and understands your plan for success.

The more detailed your plan, the more focus you'll have and the better chance you'll have of achieving your goals. The best salesperson I ever had working for me had a laser-focused daily plan. He broke the day down into hours. He accounted for every minute he spent at the office. He would prospect certain hours of the day; he would only accept calls during certain hours, and he made presentations at scheduled times. Every detail was scheduled.

A detailed plan is important because it's so easy to be distracted and thrown off course. You must commit to a plan if you want to be successful in a consistent way.

In *Think and Grow Rich*, Napoleon Hill writes, "If you can conceive it and believe it, you can achieve it." There have been many times when I've had to defend this statement from those who just don't get it. Your plan might not always work out exactly like you want in the time frame you expected, but if you are truly committed to your plan and aggressively pursue it, you will achieve your goals.

CASE STUDY

A Uniroyal Example

We first met Uniroyal Tire Corporation at a trade show on a Friday, and, unbelievably, we set our presentation for the following Wednesday. At the time, the sales cycle for the product I sold was four to five months long. (Usually, the bigger the corporation, the longer the sales cycle.) Uniroyal had never heard of our company. They were not familiar with our solution, and certainly did not know me. We did the proper qualification and preparation prior to flying across the country.

Part of my preparation included getting Uniroyal's annual report and understanding their mission statement. After reviewing both in some detail, I easily made a road map for what I hoped would be a successful sales presentation.

When we finished, the decision-maker commented that our company and Uniroyal's goals matched perfectly. This match was no accident! It was the result of doing my homework. We ended our sales presentation and had a signed corporate-wide agreement on Friday—a two-day sales cycle!

Knowing as much as you can about a potential customer creates trust and says you respect what is important to them. In the case of Uniroyal, the decision-maker saw that his company and ours shared a common philosophy. He came to this conclusion because I'd done my homework and tailored my sales presentation to highlight the similarities between Uniroyal's mission and our own.

Most representatives make the mistake of giving a canned pitch to their prospects. Believe me, such an approach will hurt you every time. It says to the prospect that you don't care enough about what you do to be prepared or that you are lazy.

In today's competitive selling environment, little things make the difference. Sometimes prospects don't realize why they choose one company over another. Customizing your presentation based on a company's mission statement might just be enough to connect honestly with the decision maker. Learn to speak the prospect's language, not your own.

CHAPTER FIVE

The Attributes of Success

The singer James Taylor says the secret of life is enjoying the passing of time. The secret of love is opening up your heart. Unfortunately, he doesn't identify the secret of success or selling. Until he does, I have discovered the attributes of success that work. In fact, I'd even suggest that you copy these attributes, then place a copy on your desk and in your briefcase, and maybe even hang one next to the bathroom mirror.

Read them daily. Think about them. Learn them. Measure yourself against them. The more successful you are, the better you'll measure up against this list.

....

THIRTEEN QUALITIES OF SUCCESSFUL SALES REPRESENTATIVES

1. COMMITMENT

2. FOCUS

3. KNOWLEDGE

4. WORK ETHIC

5. BELIEF

6. CONFIDENCE

7. Courage

8. Competitiveness

9. Creativity

10. Goals

11. Team Player

12. Preparation

13. Strategy

Many people possess some of these attributes, but those who achieve amazing results are committed to each attribute, and they consistently work to develop these attributes day after day, year after year. Make these attributes the foundation for your personal and business life and you'll go far. Salespeople, more than those in any other profession, need the discipline of these attributes to succeed on a consistent basis.

Over the years, when one of the salespeople I managed performed poorly, I have compared his actions against this list and quickly identified the problem.

1. Commitment

What are you doing to become a higher-level sales expert? Are you reading books, studying those who are successful, attending seminars, and doing all you can do to eliminate any weaknesses?

Here are some more thoughts on the subject:

Just because you go to class does not make you a student.

Just because you sing does not make you a professional singer.

Just because you have something to sell does not necessarily mean you are a professional sales person.

Just because you are in a profession does not mean that you are a professional.

Successful students, singers and sales people have developed the skill of being absorbed physically, mentally and emotionally. Being in something does not mean you'll get anything out of it. The only way you'll ever totally get the most out of it is if you are totally into it.

It takes far more than desire to succeed in order to be successful. Hard work and preparation are equally important. If you have the right attitude, if you're into sales, then the desire to work hard and prepare will come naturally. You will succeed.

2. Focus

Do you have a daily, disciplined routine you follow for which you hold yourself accountable? Are you easily distracted?

Identify your talents

Observe your mentors

Challenge yourself

Utilize your resources

Strive to make a difference

3. Knowledge

Are you doing everything you can to learn the product, the market, and how to better apply your knowledge in order to close deals?

The world's shortest sales course

1. Know your business.

2. Know your stuff.

By "stuff," I mean you should know how to employ the Quid Pro Quo sales methodology, know where you want to go, how you get there, and how you can offer tangible benefits to the customer.

4. Work ethic

Are you putting in the minimum hours, doing just what it takes to get by, or giving 110%? Are you really giving yourself the best chance for success?

5. Belief

Do you believe in yourself, the company, the products, and your ability to follow a disciplined routine? Are you doing the things to be successful even when it's hard or uncomfortable?

6. Confidence

Do you express confidence when you are selling?

Do you feel strongly that you are, indeed, helping people with the product or services you are offering? Are you confident that you can communicate to them, with a sense of urgency, the benefits of buying what you are selling?

"Nothing splendid has ever been achieved except by those who dared to believe that something inside them was superior to circumstance."

Bruce Barton (1886-1967), Advertising Executive

7. Courage

Do you have the courage to take control of the sales cycle, to say "no" to the hard things that are uncomfortable? Or are you following the path of least resistance?

8. Competitiveness

Do you take it personally when others around you are succeeding at a higher level than you are? Get in the game and compete!

"Life is not a spectator sport. If you're going to spend your whole life in the grandstand just watching what goes on, in my opinion, you're wasting your life."

Jackie Robinson, Baseball player and manager

9. Creativity

How creative are you in helping prospects overcome objections? Are you being creative in your prospecting methods? It's important to think "out of the box" and be creative if you are going to get ahead.

10. Goals

Have you established specific goals for yourself and written them down? Have you detailed the tasks to achieve these goals? How often do you refer to this written list? The most likely way to reach a goal is to aim not at the goal itself, but at the more ambitious goal beyond it.

"When I got cut from the varsity team as a sophomore in high school, I learned something. I learned that I never wanted to feel that bad again. I knew I never wanted to have that taste in my mouth, that hole in my stomach. So I set a goal and committed to becoming a starter on the varsity."

Michael Jordan, Basketball player, owner, and manager

11. Team player

Are you sharing information and receiving knowledge from those around you who are succeeding at a level different from your own?

12. Preparation

Are you prepared for every task, every sales call, every presentation? How prepared are you to come to work each day and set a new one-day record?

13. Strategy

Are you implementing a strategy to generate more qualified prospects? Do you settle for just calling company supplied leads? Do you have a strategy for every prospect you pursue?

The World's Greatest Sales Strategy
by Advertising Guru Leo Burnett

Don't tell me how good you make it:

tell me how good it makes me when I use it.

At the end of the day, how you embody the attributes listed above will determine if you succeed or fail. If you make adhering to this list part of your strategy, your earnings will increase dramatically. Your new success will manifest itself in a new, more confident attitude, which in turn will generate even more success.

The Bottom Line

Not everyone will be able to adopt all the principles in this book. Not everyone who earns a living in sales is successful either. In his book *Executive Speeches*, Richard L. Weaver says:

"Face it. Nobody owes you a living. What you achieve or fail to achieve in your lifetime is directly related to what you do or fail to do.

"People don't choose their parents or childhood but you can choose your own direction.

"Everyone has problems and obstacles to overcome, but that too is relative to each individual.

"Nothing is carved into stone. You can change anything in your life if you want to badly enough.

"Excuses are for losers. Those who take responsibility for their actions are the real winners in life.

"Winners meet life's challenge head on, knowing there are no guarantees and they give all they've got.

"Never think it's too early to begin. Time plays no favorites and will pass whether you act or not."

CHAPTER SIX

The Fundamentals

With sales, executing fundamentals is the key to success. Fundamentals provide the foundation you build on. As long as you have a firm foundation, you can continue to build and expand your skills.

General Colin Powell once said, "There are no secrets to success: don't waste time looking for them. Success is the result of perfection, hard work, learning from failure, loyalty to those with whom you work, and persistence."

Bond with Your Prospect

Building a bond with your prospect is at the core of the fundamentals for successful selling. The foundation of Quid Pro Quo selling is creating a give-and-take relationship. Rapport is typically a by-product of that relationship. Sometimes the relationship and rapport is easily established and is entirely natural. Other times, you have to work hard for it.

To build rapport, you should be friendly and genuinely interested in your prospect. The following list displays the key attributes needed to create the give-and-take relationships, which will enable you to be successful on a constant basis.

Seven Ways to Get People to Like You

1. Be confident and enthusiastic
2. Be sincerely interested in others

3. Talk about the other person's interests
4. Use the other person's name
5. Give compliments
6. Be a good listener
7. Make the other person feel important

You are Responsible

If a company were a football team, you—its sales rep—would be the quarterback. You are responsible for prospecting, qualifying, setting proper expectations, selling the company, understanding the alternatives, reporting, administrative duties, closing and, in general, running and controlling the activity as if you were running your own franchise. Beyond this, you also have to understand every prospect's buying motives, business issues and personal situation in regards to your product or services.

Sell to Individuals, Not Companies

Another fundamental point to remember—and one that is overlooked many times by sales people—is that you sell to individuals with their own personal agendas, not to companies. I have never seen "the company" buy or write a check for something. A company is merely a group of individuals with stresses, issues and concerns like those you face every day. When you understand that you're always selling to individuals with problems similar to yours, and when you adjust your sales approach accordingly, you will become much more effective.

Ask Yourself, "So What?"

Whenever you speak to your prospects, you should imagine them shaking their heads and saying, "So what!" as you speak. You should picture these words written across their foreheads. Prospects say, "So what?" when they have no idea why the sales person is telling them whatever they're telling them.

Know Your Prospect's Issues

Another fundamental point for success is to always keep in mind the prospect's issues. Speak to the specific needs of each prospect. Don't ever give a presentation or product demo before the prospect understands why she needs your product and how it will solve her problems.

Never assume that the prospect knows what you're talking about or that he understands each point you're trying to make. Don't even assume that he understands what your objective is. Talk only in terms your prospect can understand and relate to.

Make Features, Benefits, and Differentiation Statements

Selling the features of your product is fundamental to your success. Most product evaluations are sold by what I refer to as the "Feature Bee." A Feature Bee is just like a spelling bee: the competing sales people line up, and the prospect asks each one if his product has a certain feature. If it doesn't, then that sales person has to sit down. The last sales person standing wins the business.

Of course, evaluations are not actually done this way, but far too many sales representatives pitch their products as if they were in a Feature Bee. They hope the buzz will cover up the fact that they don't have particularly good sales skills.

A better way to sell is to use the Quid Pro Quo approach and relate each feature to a benefit. Why? Because no one really cares about features. Prospects only care about the benefit they get from owning products that have features that will serve their needs. Features by themselves sell nothing. Benefits and relating them sell.

Never assume that the prospect will understand how a certain feature is going to benefit her. Your job is to ask enough qualifying questions so that you'll know precisely how to relate each benefit to a prospect's business and personal issues. You should also demonstrate in your benefit statements how others within the company will be able to take advantage of any given benefit. By doing so, you'll be helping the prospect envision how your product is going to make her situation much better.

Differentiate your product or service from any alternatives. Always tie a feature to a benefit to a differentiation statement. Prospects generally consider multiple options before buying anything. They often get confused when confronted by all the choices available.

When you make a differentiation statement, your goal is to separate your product from all the alternatives. You must clearly point out why the benefits and features of your product are superior based on the prospect's needs and different from those offered by the competition.

When you tie features, benefits, and differentiation statements to a prospect's personal issue, it will separate you in every way from competitors. Doing so will make it easy for your prospect to buy from you.

CHAPTER SEVEN

The Most Important Work You'll Ever Do

Prospecting—and qualifying—are the most important steps in sales success. You need prospects to move forward. Unfortunately, prospecting is also the most tedious and thankless part of the sales process. You must be willing to stay focused and motivated even when it's tough going.

The goal of prospecting is simple: to generate leads for new business. This is extremely important because most companies find that the largest percentage of their growth comes from new business rather than from an increase in sales from existing clients. Consequently, prospecting is critical to your success. It's very difficult to grow and succeed without new opportunities. Fortunately, there are many ways to generate new leads.

Prospecting and Cold Calling

Prospecting is spreading the good word about your company and products or service. The biggest obstacle that you usually have to overcome is your prospects' unfamiliarity with your company and the products or services you provide. Ideally, everyone in a company is responsible for finding prospects. Since self-generated leads and referrals are always the best contacts, however, you should always be looking for prospecting opportunities in order to realize the maximum results from your efforts.

If you think that you usually put in a good hard day, you should take a second and reflect. How many good contacts–the people who could and should purchase your product or service—did you make? If you talked to fewer than fifteen or twenty people, there's a good chance you spent too much time shuffling papers. As a sales representative, you must be honest with yourself. To be successful, you must identify your strengths and weaknesses.

Cold calling, an uninvited call by you to a prospective client to introduce yourself and your company, is the prospecting tool most used by sales people. This remains one of the most difficult and challenging activities for many salespeople to perform consistently. It's far better to work hard to acquire referrals (which are leads) than to make cold calls. Why? Because it's far easier to sell to a referred prospect with an identified problem that you can solve than to convert a cold call into a sale.

Leads vs. Cold Calling

Leads	Cold Calling
Usually returns calls	Often doesn't return calls
Listens respectfully	Are not sure they should listen
Views you as an expert	Views you as a typical salesman

Remember this: everyone knows someone to whom you could sell. The people you are calling on most likely have relationships with other people who would benefit from your offering. At the end of each call, always ask this simple question: "Who else do you know that I should talk to?" The question is easy to ask and is worth millions of dollars.

Why? Because referrals are absolutely the best leads. Think about your mindset when you call a good referral. You are more confident, you have instant creditability with the prospect, and you usually know something about their circumstances. With a referral, you start out ahead of the game.

Marketing

Virtually every company markets their products in order to generate prospects. Your marketing program should create focused, high-quality, innovative communications and produce channels to generate the highest possible level of awareness and demand for your products. I am sure your company is spending a considerable amount of money on programs that will generate new opportunities for you. Don't make the mistake of sitting back and waiting on leads! Regardless of the environment, you are in control of your destiny. The best plan is to create opportunities for yourself.

Creating Your Own Marketing and Promotion Strategy

As part of your Franchise Plan, you should include a section for marketing and promotion strategies. Specifically, it should focus on lead-generation strategies for your territory. Most companies' marketing programs include:

1. Collateral Materials
    Level I overview brochures
    Demo CD's
2. Direct Mail
    Mailing lists
    Newsletters
3. Trade Shows
    Industry trade shows
4. Channels

Alignment with organizations that will promote your solution, or even sell it with and for you.

Differentiation

Certain aspects of your product will be unique in the industry. This uniqueness should be understood and clearly articulated to your prospect. Be sure to frame this uniqueness in terms of a specific benefit to your prospect. You should create a list of all the unique aspects of your solution. Here's an example:

- A Windows® based system that is easy to use.
- Training and support to ensure your success.
- Enhancement programs with more than 600 different options already set up.
- System-generated, easy-to-follow signals that tell clients exactly what decisions to make.
- A lifetime warranty on the product.
- 100% customer satisfaction.

It's also important to differentiate specifically from the other market alternatives. By concentrating on your products' unique qualities, while understanding your area and your prospect's needs, it's easy to find new sales opportunities. Prospecting and differentiation must occur at every step of the sales process.

Goals

When it comes to marketing, your goals are pretty straightforward. You must create an awareness of your company, your solution and yourself. Once this awareness is established, it'll be easier for you to find prospects and convert them into clients.

Clients = sales = volume = commissions

Don't be satisfied with merely reaching the quota set by your sales manager. The most likely way to reach a goal is to aim not at the goal itself but at some ambitious goal beyond it.

Marketing Activities

When combined, all your marketing activities will generate the leads which will increase your sales. Decide which activities are applicable to your business. Not performing all these activities is an option. Not performing any of these activities is not an option. Take control of your level of success. Don't be afraid to invest in your success.

Don't be penny-wise and pound foolish. If I offered you a $5 bill for your $1 bill, would you take it? Of course you would. You need to have the same attitude when it comes to spending money on yourself in your territory to achieve the sales goals you have written in your personal business plan for the year.

An old Spanish proverb says, "It's not the same to talk of the bulls as to be in the bullring." This essentially means that if you talk the talk, you've got to walk the walk. You have to take responsibility for your opportunity. Expect nothing except that which you can generate yourself. You are responsible for your own success.

Lead Generation

Direct Mail

Direct mail could be the cornerstone of your marketing plan. These mailings should be done regularly to inform people about your company. In addition, they should include web cast invitations, seminar invitations, and other invitations. One part of your mailing should always invite prospects to take action (attend a web cast, come to a seminar, or call for a demo). The remainder should address the specific hot-button solutions that your product provides.

Creating pieces that will move prospects to action is a high priority. Always follow up immediately to any responses.

Continuity

It's important to standardize and coordinate the message and theme of any direct mailings or ad campaigns that you initiate. Lack of continuity confuses customers. When they see different messages and themes, they may not associate them with the same company. With your limited marketing budget, you can't afford to have this happen. Each ad or piece of literature must have maximum impact. Continuity among these items will strengthen your image and allow you to better differentiate yourself. You may need your marketing department's approval before you proceed because there may be legal issues about which you are unaware.

Telemarketing

From time to time, you may be given an overwhelming number of inquiries from your corporate headquarters. In this case, many successful representatives hire a telemarketing person to initially qualify the leads. Once the lead is qualified, you have the best opportunity to work toward closing business. Using telemarketing enables you to focus on your active prospects.

Another use of telemarketing is to cold call within your territory to jump start business. A telemarketing person could also update your database. Occasionally, your company will provide telemarketing, but I've found it's more beneficial to employ your own help.

One person who worked for me used telemarketing to get prospects to attend his seminars. Why would he do this? Because he got about 80% of his business from hosting seminars, and because he closed 50% of the prospects that attended.

He got every possible list of names from the area where the seminar was to be held and had a couple of people call those names on the list. They were paid $25 for each person who attended and $50 for each person who attended and bought. It was a win-win situation because the person earned considerably more when the prospects bought.

Note: There's a great deal of rejection inherent in telemarketing or telesales. At least 90% of all calls do not result in a sale. Since this is the case, you may initially want to hire a part-time person to do the calling for you. You'll be able to spend your time on more productive activities while benefiting from the work of your part-time helper. But always remember that rejection hurts, and you must continually support your helper with words of encouragement.

Lead Exchange Programs

Building awareness in the market for yourself and your product is an ongoing process. Cooperating with other firms on a lead exchange program or a co-marketing agreement can quickly generate qualified leads. Your goal should be to establish at least several working agreements that supply qualified prospects.

Lead exchange programs are easiest to set up when there is a win-win situation established. Everyone, regardless of the business they're in, likes to get referrals or leads. You should consider all sources that could bring you good opportunities.

··

TO CONDUCT YOUR AWARENESS CAMPAIGN, DO THE

FOLLOWING:

1. COORDINATE YOUR ACTIONS AND THOUGHTS WITH CORPORATE

MANAGEMENT.

2. Contact the potential firms you have had or want to have relationships with.

3. Supply them with sales brochures, demo CDs, and whatever other collateral materials you have available. This will give them something to show their clients.

4. Add the firms to your database so they can receive regular mailings from your company.

5. Maintain regular contact with these resources.

Marketing Ideas to Consider

Generally, you have to spend a little money to make a lot of money. Place ads in local publications or industry publications at your own expense. Most companies won't expect you to do this. But remember, you're not interested in doing the minimum you need to do to get by. Your goal is to maximize your opportunity and set a new, higher standard in your organization. That's how you get ahead.

Your ad will obviously promote your product, solution, and company. Since you've paid for it, you want it to promote yourself as well. Each ad needs to point out at least one thing about yourself that will give you credibility with the prospects who read it. It should also indicate how the prospects can reach you directly.

Newsletter

Create a newsletter for your customers informing them of the exciting things that are happening at your company and encouraging them to call you with new prospects. Identify new companies who have joined your team of customers. Have some of your customers write a testimonial for you. Many people enjoy reading how others are using your product, and they may learn something new to help them better utilize the product. Many people will gladly write an article for you.

Collateral Material

When sending collateral material to your clients, pick specific regional issues that you can relate to your product or the problem it solves in the marketplace. Use any materials your company has available to you, and create your own by copying articles you read in the paper, magazines, and other sources.

Sending an article to a prospect that relates to her specific issues does a couple of things. First, it lets the prospect know you are in tune with both the industry and her issue. Second, it gives you credibility from both a personal standpoint and a business standpoint.

If you regularly send relevant material that addresses a prospect's issues, when that prospect is ready to buy, he'll generally buy from you, the person who kept him informed. Each time you send out something to your prospect, be sure to include a short handwritten note explaining why the article is relevant and how you are available to help. Create a direct mail piece and pro actively cover your area.

Internal Communications

Everyone needs to know his company's story and to be held account-able for some level of lead generation. If you have a service component to your product, it's always a good idea to enlist the help of the post-sales team servicing your accounts. Typically, these people are out in the field and have many opportunities to help you generate new prospects. You'll want to let them know you appreciate what they are doing.

Research Your Area

It's important to get involved in your community. You should look for every possible opportunity to gather groups together to present your product. You'll want to align yourself with leaders in your area. You need to get to know people who have a large network of contacts who can help you sell your product.

This should be the cornerstone of your self-marketing plan. Networking works off the premise that everybody knows some body. A lot of sales people understand the concept of networking but usually only apply it when they are looking for a job. I can say just about every opportunity I was presented with in my life has come from someone else alerting me to the opportunity, introducing me to someone who knew someone else who had an opportunity, or referring me to someone or some place. Stop a minute and think. Is the same true for you? If this is the case, why don't you make a focused effort to build a network? There are a few reasons why networking doesn't work for most sales people:

- They want immediate gratification
- They don't want to make the investment
- They have never tried it before
- They don't understand the first rule of networking
- They don't know how to or have never measured the results

Want Immediate Gratification?

Don't we all want immediate gratification, regardless of what we are doing? In most cases I think the answer to that question is, "Yes." This need or want for immediate gratification is compounded when we enter the world of sales. Sales people are under the gun for consistent and immediate results. They don't have time to invest in much of anything if it is not going to bear fruit right away. The average job span for a sales person in technology is 18 months. Every 18 months, on average, sales people switch jobs. If they don't produce the results and meet the company's expectations, they are asked to leave. Or the other side of the coin is that the company has oversold the sales person in the interview process and they choose to leave. Either way, who has time for networking? Trust me, this thinking is extremely flawed. Below is a vision that I hope stays in your brain.

Networking is your chain saw! Sometime we get so wrapped up in quotas, unqualified prospects or meetings, we don't see the obvious, which might be right in front of us.

One thing that makes no sense whatsoever but we are guilty of doing from time to time is following the classic definition of insanity. (Doing the same thing over and over again and expecting a different result.) I see this all the time with sales people. They work their tail off and do not achieve the expected results they were working toward. The question that must be asked is, "What are you going to do differently next month?" Typically the answer that comes back is just more of the same actions that didn't work the month before. This makes no sense, even though we have all done this. If something is not working, you're going to have to make some adjustments to see a change. Committing to a disciplined networking plan might be just the change you need.

Making the Investment

You are a committed professional in the world of sales. If you don't make the investment, who will? When a sales person leaves a company she has to turn in all related marketing materials, her laptop, credit card, and a host of other things. But the network she keeps.

Your network is yours! It stays with you your entire career, regardless of what you are doing, your role, or the company you work for. No one can take it away from you. The people in your network are working with you as an individual. They have bought in to you and the relationship you have established with them. As long as you continue to invest and work with your network, it will never leave. I can't think of anything you could invest in that would be more valuable to a successful career.

The Essential Rule of Networking

Now that you understand just how valuable networking can be to your self-marketing plan, it is critical to understand the rules. Make a list of all the people you can think of who could potentially help you uncover some opportunities.

Make sure you write these names down or, better yet, create a spreadsheet. We'll come back to the reason for a spreadsheet. Here's the issue that throws most sales people under the networking bus. The first rule of networking: Successful networking is all about helping other people.

Revisit your list of potential networking partners. Do you know how you can help them? Creating the list now becomes a little more challenging. If you are wondering how you might help your potential networking partners, remember they will want the same things you want: introductions, referrals or help. Sometime you have to give to get, and that is fine when it comes to networking.

One reason for the spreadsheet is you will want to measure how much time you spend with any given member in your network, how much assistance or leads you have provided to them and what ROI (return on investment) you have received from the relationship. The goal is to build partnerships. You have to measure your time and the results you are receiving from everyone in your network. This is key to your success.

Measure the Results

Go back to your networking spreadsheet to measure the results. The formula to measure marketing activities: TIME + ACTIVITY = RESULTS. This is a pretty simple but powerful formula for success. The time you invest in any activity has to achieve the results you are looking for. If it doesn't, then replace that activity or spend a lot less time pursuing that activity.There are many people who are professional networkers. They meet, help lots of people, work hard, but then forget they have to sell something too.

Three Categories for Your Spreadsheet

In your spreadsheet, divide your people into three different categories. The first group is experts or mavens. These are people that the industry recognizes as "the voice." If they promote it, then it must be good.

The second group is connectors. One out of a thousand know a hundred people. Connectors know lots of people in various industries and walks of life. Connectors are powerful because they know other connectors.

The third category is sales people. These are non-competing sales people who are calling on your accounts. Of course you know how to help these people and they know how to help you. Create a network and leverage your contacts.

You will want to eliminate the time you are spending helping people in your network who do not reciprocate. You'll have to measure this regularly to know which people are good partners and which need to be taken off your list.

Tracking the Profitability of Your Contacts

Reference Source	Type	Actual Number of Referrals	Actual Number Engaged	Actual Number in Pipeline	Actual Numbe Closed
Mallory	SR	6	3	2	1
Lichter	C	7	1	5	1
Blankenship	SR	9	3	4	2
Personal Referral Totals		18	7	11	4
Business Chronicle		10	5	7	3
Monster		23	12	11	0
Headhunter		17	5	10	2
HotJobs		19	19	0	0
Trade Shows		11	2	9	0
R3 Personal Contacts		8	6	1	1
Other Sources Totals		85	49	38	6
Total Referrals/ Leads		103	53	47	10
% advanced		100%	55%	43%	2%

Target Number of Referrals	Target Number Engaged	Target Number in Pipeline	Target Number Closed	Projected Dates
8	4	4	0	
5	2	2	1	
8	1	5	3	
21	7	11	4	
9	8	0	1	
15	1	4	9	
30	20	5	5	
12	0	3	9	
19	9	6	4	
10	6	0	4	
95	44	18	32	
116	52	29	36	
100%	44%	25%	31%	

The Mercedes-Benz Connection

A friend of mine, a newcomer in town, wanted to get established in the community as a financial consultant. It was critical for him to know as many influential people as possible. One of the first things he did was make a visit to the local Mercedes-Benz dealership.

He went in and asked for the owner, cordially introducing himself and letting him know right up front why he was there. He used all the bonding skills he had. During the discussion, the owner tried to interest my friend in a car. He even let him drive a new Mercedes for the weekend, as dealerships often do. The consultant gladly accepted this offer but was up front about the fact that he wasn't in the auto market until his business increased. He drove the car and returned it after the weekend. He thanked the owner, and again stated his position.

You'd think that my friend's objective—making contact and establishing a level of rapport—had been met and that would be the end of it. However, my friend spent $60, and went one step further. He placed an ad in the local newspaper which read, "I want to thank Mr. Jones from Jones Mercedes-Benz for such a pleasant experience. Mr. Jones was kind, generous and it was a pleasure to deal with him. I would like to recommend him personally and his dealership to everyone."

Mr. Jones became excited when he saw the ad in the paper. He called the consultant and thanked him, telling him that no one in his twenty years in business had ever done anything like that before. Then he asked, "Is there anything I can do for you?" Of course, this is exactly what my friend was hoping. For $60 and a 30-minute meeting, he now had someone on his team to help him build his business.

What creative things can you do to build your business?

Direct Mail Follow-Up

Make sure that you have an efficient method to follow up on direct mail and call inquiries. It's not enough to just send out e-mail blasts, fax blasts or any other direct communication. You need to follow up. I've seen representatives put together some outstanding pieces that call prospects to action. They hit all the prospects' hot buttons. Unfortunately, a lot of time and effort was wasted because the representatives sat back and waited for the phone to ring.

Don't fall in love with your marketing material. Believe me, it won't do great things on its own. You must have a call-back plan any time you send anything out. Assume your information will not be read unless you follow up in a timely fashion. As a consultant, I've had to stress this point with companies over and over again.

....

WHEN IT COMES TO DIRECT MAIL, THERE ARE TWO SIMPLE

RULES TO FOLLOW:

1. HAVE A CALL-BACK PLAN.

2. DON'T LET MORE THAN THREE DAYS PASS BEFORE YOU MAKE YOUR

CALLS.

Remember, you personally don't have to make the calls. That's what telemarketers are for. If you don't have telemarketers then you do need to make the calls yourself.

Events Management

Create opportunities that will give you and your company the most exposure. Be as creative as possible. Dinners for small groups can be a very effective means of generating sales. If you invite six to twelve people for a dinner, most restaurants will provide you with a private room. Many people give a short presentation before the meal. After your presentation, sit down, answer questions, continue selling, and enjoy the meal with your prospects. Of course, you want to make sure the entire group is properly qualified before you invite them.

Hosting small dinners is also an effective way to make yourself known in your territory and to establish contacts who can pass on referrals. Some representatives I know go the extra mile and hire a limo to pick up attendees. Who would turn down a free dinner with a limo pick up? Very few of us would. This is an excellent way to set yourself apart at a reasonable cost.

I'm also a big fan of seminars. You can gather large groups of people together for a very low cost. Time is the most valuable asset you have. Seminars enable you to sell directly to the largest number of people in the least amount of time.

In today's markets, prospects have so many choices it's hard to keep up. This is especially true if you are selling technology. Seminars enable you to educate and sell prospects simultaneously. The Quid Pro Quo approach will enable you to educate prospects so that they'll want to buy from you.

CASE STUDY

Leveraging Knowledge

Offset Atlanta is a successful commercial printing firm based outside of Atlanta, Georgia. It is part of a nationwide network of printing companies call Premiere Printing. We trained their local staff on the Quid Pro Quo selling approach as well as have a productive consulting relationship.

The issues were similar to many organizations today. They were facing increasing competition in their market. In the greater Atlanta area alone there are approximately 300 commercial printers. This is a lot of competitors for such a small geography. The team at Offset Atlanta wanted to be able to differentiate themselves from other printers.

After going through the courses, regular follow up and reinforcement, the team was seeing great results. Still they wanted more.

Offset Atlanta had been in the Atlanta market for years and was full of expertise. We decided to leverage that expertise as a way to differentiate from all the other commercial printers.

To leverage this knowledge, we decided to hold monthly "Lunch & Learns." The idea was to invite prospects and customers to a one-hour monthly lunch presentation. The Offset Atlanta team would invite print buyers, designers, marketers and other potential customers to come to the luncheons. We selected 12 compelling educational topics about different aspects of printing. They even went so far as to invite other complimentary vendors to offer information. This not only enhanced the topics, but these vendors also sprang for buying the lunches for everyone. Someone from Offset Atlanta would kick off the lunch with a brief introduction and then jump right into the educational topic of the month.

It was easy to get people to attend since they usually go out to lunch for an hour anyway. Plus they were gaining valuable knowledge. With each passing month, the "Lunch & Learns" became increasingly popular with the audience quickly reaching about 50 people each month. Soon the companies in the area started to perceive that Offset Atlanta was different. They were mavens in the printing industry by the mere fact they were holding these "Lunch & Learn" seminars.

To this day Offset Atlanta still uses "Lunch & Learns" as their marketing plan. It has been so successful for them, every company in the nationwide network of Premiere Printing companies is required to hold a monthly "Lunch & Learn."

Alternate Channels

Without a doubt, you need to have as many people as possible selling your product for you. You should always be on the lookout for other people and companies to be part of your prospecting program.

Forming partnerships with other sales representatives, companies, and professional and social organizations can leverage your efforts. Find representatives and companies that have the same target market you have for your product. (Most of them won't be direct competitors.) You can create a win/win situation by exchanging opportunities. If you can find an organization that can represent your product in a professional manner and acquire new customers for you, by all means set up a relationship that works for all parties.

Strategic Relations

There are many ways to find alternate-channel partners. One is to survey your customers to see if, through a partnership, they can help you promote your product.

You can set up a formal referral arrangement, utilizing a co-marketing or co-selling agreement. More casual arrangements often work well between individuals. The downside of corporate agreements is that they usually take a long time to put together, and with all the effort, the results are often mixed. I prefer the arrangements between individuals. Control your own destiny and make arrangements that provide incentives to customers who work with you.

CHAPTER EIGHT

Qualifying

When interviewed for jobs, most sales people are asked this question: "What is the most important part of the sales cycle?" More times than not the answer comes back, "The close." Wrong.

Along with prospecting, qualification is the most important part of the sales cycle. You can't close an unqualified prospect. Many people would like a five-bedroom beach house, but if you were a real-estate salesperson, it would make no sense for you to spend a day showing these beautiful homes to someone who couldn't afford them, no matter how good a closer or how beautiful the houses. A prospect without the means is unqualified and therefore is not a prospect. You need to be sure you are talking to the decision maker.

With every opportunity, sales people must make sure that time and resources are spent effectively. Proper qualification of your prospects will enable you to decide which ones deserve your time and attention.

God gave you two ears and one mouth for a reason: listen! Too many times, sales people get excited and skip the step of asking good, open-ended questions about the prospect's buying motives and personal situation. These situations end up having premature elaboration. Don't let this happen to you. Premature elaboration is when a sales person comes out and starts to sell before learning everything he needs to about the opportunity. Premature elaboration is never a good thing.

Sales people who make this mistake assume too much because they think they've heard it all before. If you're talking more than your prospect, you're hurting yourself and not getting any closer to the sale. Talking more than listening will cost you a lot of business. Is there anything you need to know that would help point out why your prospect should purchase your product? If your prospects are not buying and not giving you valid reasons why not, then there is a good chance that you've not discovered their real objections. The sales representative must ask enough open-ended questions to help the prospect feel comfortable and communicate genuine interest.

Far too many representatives ask a couple of high level questions, hear what they want to hear ("happy ears"), and rush into a product demonstration. Why do they follow this path? Because the senior management team has drilled into them that the product is so good that all they have to do is show it to prospects and they'll buy.

Falling into this trap will cost you more than you might think. Proper qualification of your prospects will enable you to determine which ones deserve a product demonstration.

CASE STUDY

ShipXact

After a frustrating day of prospecting, my phone rang. When I answered it the gentlemen on the other end said, "Bob, you were referred to me as an expert in sales strategies, sales approach, and training. We are looking for consulting, training, and an organization to help us increase our revenues. How can you help us?" Wow, I almost fell out of my chair! If I had happy ears what I might have heard was that someone from my referral network gave me an over the top endorsement. I could have assumed the selling was done.

At this point what would you have done? I think most sales people would have started verbally "throwing up" on the guy on the phone. They would have fallen all over themselves telling exactly what they have to offer in each one of the areas the gentlemen inquired about. I'll even admit it took everything I had not to start elaborating on our expertise, but that would have been premature and could have cost me.

Instead I restrained myself and asked him to tell me about his company. He gave me more detail on their needs, what is driving them, time frames and cost expectations. As much as I wanted to bag the opportunity, it was prudent to first get answers to the selling questions. The person on the other end of the phone was more than happy to share with me all the information I wanted. He went on for 20-30 minutes. Every word he spoke was like putting money in the bank. He was telling me everything I needed to know to satisfy him that Sales Builders was really the only alternative he could reasonably consider. With each word the target got closer and more in focus. At this point neither a shot gun nor a rifle was needed. Putting my emotional enthusiasm on hold for 30 minutes made selling this opportunity extremely easy.

The other important point to note is that by asking some important questions, I could qualify this account fully to insure it was indeed a good prospect for us. It would not have served either company to pursue an opportunity that was not a good fit for either one of us.

I witness sales people all the time trying to jam a square peg in a round hole. Once in a while they are successful, but this almost never makes for a satisfied client. Worse, they spend lots of time and money pursuing an opportunity that in the end, they do not win. This will absolutely have a negative effect on your sales productivity.

Can You Sell Me a Pencil?

Have you ever been in an interview and the person across the desk cleverly asked you to sell them a pencil? What do you think 90% of all salespeople do when asked to take on this challenge? What would you do?

Most sales people instantly start explaining to the interviewer all the positive aspects of a pencil, and they do this in ten seconds or less! Premature elaboration generally occurs when an excited or abrupt prospect asks representatives to show them the product.

The correct way to prevent premature elaboration is to start asking the right questions. "Mr. Interviewer, what exactly are you looking for in a pencil? Do you prefer wooden or mechanical? Do you want one with or without an eraser? How will you be using this pencil? How important is status to you, or is price your top consideration? How will you be evaluating the different pencils you're considering?" And so forth. After you've sorted out the answers, it becomes very easy to sell the pencil to your interviewer.

Since qualification is basic to Quid Pro Quo selling, I've never understood why salespeople regularly waste time working unqualified accounts or building relationships with people who offer unqualified opportunities.

I've learned that it's always better to ask the hard questions up front. It's better to find out sooner rather than later if the prospect you're working with is really qualified. If you wait until the end of the sales cycle, you will risk wasting all the time and effort you've put into your prospect.

Unfortunately, salespeople seem to have a natural fear of qualifying early in the sales cycle. If you understand this fear, you'll become a better salesperson, and you'll understand why it's important to get the answers to the qualifying questions early in the sales cycle.

....

BASICS OF QUALIFICATION

THERE ARE FOUR BASIC STEPS TO QUALIFICATION.

1. THE PROSPECT HAS A NEED YOU CAN MEET.

2. THE PROSPECT HAS A COMPELLING REASON TO BUY.

3. THE PROSPECT HAS A SENSE OF URGENCY.

4. THE PROSPECT IS WILLING TO CONSIDER CHANGE.

If the prospect doesn't reveal these qualifications initially, it is the sales person's job to discover them. If you are not successful in doing so, the person is certainly not a qualified prospect. Most salespeople are guilty of having prospects who do not meet these basic criteria of qualification. Why? The salesperson's biggest fear is coming to work and admitting that the true qualified pipeline is blank. It is easier to find an opportunity who may at some point possibly buy something than it is to find someone who meets the basics of qualification and will buy.

Hold your prospects to the basics. If they do not stack up, spend your time finding qualified opportunities that will generate the results you want.

Early Qualification

To confirm whether or not the prospect is qualified, ask the "W" questions (what, why, when, and who).

What will they do? What need does the prospect have that can be met by your product or solution? Can you clearly articulate those needs? Why? Why would the prospect be willing to spend "x" dollars for your product?

When will they do it? When does the prospect plan to change his current situation? Implementation, not the close date, is the key, because it is the purpose behind the buying decision. It will tell you if the customer has a sense of urgency.

Who are the decision makers? Who will make the decision to buy? Have they made buying decisions in the past?

Who are the decision influencers who can bring pressure to bear (positive or negative) on the person who will make the final decision?

Who in the above list have you called on? It should be everyone.

Do not perform a product walk-through or presentation until all parties are present.

Bold, Direct Questions

Using the qualifying questions, you need only two personal attributes to qualify properly. The first is confidence. The second is good questioning skills that can create confidence.

The amount of information you can collect in advance, prior to a demonstration, will vary for each sale. A wealth of information can be gathered by phone. Don't be shy or afraid. All you have to do is ask. You may not get all the answers you'd like, but you definitely won't get any if you don't ask. Answers will help you steer your pitch so it's targeted to the prospect's specific issues.

Qualification Via Telephone

In many cases, you can qualify someone in a telephone conversation. The following sample telephone qualifying questions should be used as a template. As a general rule, there's nothing that you can't ask a prospect on the phone. However, I've found many sales representatives have the misconception that they have to be face-to-face before they can ask a lot of good qualifying questions.

SAMPLE TELEPHONE QUALIFYING QUESTIONS

- WHAT WILL BE THE MOST IMPORTANT PART OF YOUR EVALUATION?

- HOW DOES YOUR CURRENT SITUATION AFFECT YOU?

- WHAT ARE THE LIMITATIONS YOU SEE?

- WHO ELSE IS AFFECTED BY THESE LIMITATIONS?

- WHAT ARE YOU DOING TO RESOLVE THE ISSUE?

- WHAT IS YOUR TIME FRAME FOR A DECISION?

- WHO, OTHER THAN YOURSELF, WILL BE INVOLVED IN THE DECISION?

- WHAT KEEPS YOU AWAKE AT NIGHT IN REGARDS TO THIS ISSUE?

IF YOU ARE SELLING A PRODUCT OR SERVICE OF A TECHNICAL

NATURE, ASK THE FOLLOWING:

- HAVE YOU USED TECHNOLOGY TO HELP YOU BE MORE EFFICIENT IN

OTHER AREAS OF YOUR LIFE?

- DO YOU BELIEVE TECHNOLOGY CAN HELP YOU MAKE BETTER DECISIONS?

Open-ended questions are ones that cannot be answered with a yes or a no. They force your prospect to talk, which is always your objective.

When qualifying prospects, you should position yourself as the sales consultant or advisor, always staying inside the guidelines of the company. You want prospects to understand the opportunity you are offering them and that you are trying to help them solve problems.

....

TEN CRITERIA FOR PROSPECTS

WHAT A PROSPECT MUST DO TO QUALIFY HIMSELF TO PARTICIPATE IN THE

SALES CYCLE.

1. TO LISTEN.

2. TO EXPRESS DESIRE FOR A SOLUTION.

3. TO COMMIT TO CHANGING HABITS.

4. TO AGREE TO EXPLORE YOUR PRODUCT AS A POTENTIAL SOLUTION.

5. TO SHARE HIS SITUATION AND ISSUES.

6. TO SHARE HIS DECISION CRITERIA.

7. TO SHARE HIS CONCERNS.

8. TO AGREE TO A PLAN TO BUY.

9. TO DECIDE IF IT IS POSSIBLE TO SOLVE HIS PROBLEMS.

10. TO ACCEPT RESPONSIBILITY FOR HIS ISSUES.

Why Don't Sales Representatives Qualify?

There are two reasons why sales reps don't qualify their prospects and lapse into working unqualified prospects. The first is tactical. Salespeople don't want to offend a prospect by asking questions about decision making, spending habits, and investment strategies early on during a call.

The second and primary reason is psychological. The typical salesperson wants to be liked, and most salespeople are very likable. Unfortunately, it's more comfortable for most salespeople to build a relationship with the person by simply responding to their questions vs. asking them qualifying questions, which they fear may alienate the prospect. They want to make friends first.

CASE STUDY

Don't Copy Xerox

When I first started my career in software sales, my manager took me by the hand to show me how to sell. Our product was Enterprise Resource Planning (ERP) software, which we hoped to sell to Xerox. This software usually comes with a six-figure license fee and has a long sales cycle. My manager was a confident, well-disciplined West Point graduate who was sure he knew the right procedures. He let me know his every thought and move throughout this entire sales cycle. His contact in this account loved him. He would gladly give him time, talk for hours about anything and enjoyed his company. The end of the quarter came and Xerox was on my manager's list as a definite closing prospect.

Unfortunately, my mentor forgot to sell to the other people making the recommendations to the decision maker, and he did not qualify his prospect, now a friend, thoroughly enough. The result? Xerox bought from the competition. My sales manager should have qualified early and throughout the selling cycle.

The Xerox contact wrote a note to my manager detailing how great a guy he was, how professional and so on. The worst part was the line that said, "You were the best sales person I have ever had call on me."

With a bit more than youthful impishness, I asked my manager, "How much do you get paid for coming in second place in a software evaluation?" You know the answer too. Don't fall into the trap of failing to qualify everyone in the decision making process.

CHAPTER NINE

Qualifying the Organizational Chart

Once you've gotten to the decision-maker, it's important to understand the company's organizational chart. Why? Because it's crucial to understand the interpersonal relationships between the players in the organization. All companies are political, and being aware of the political environment can mean the difference between winning or losing a sale. You should create an organizational chart for every prospect and current customer.

Regardless of the titles used by any particular company, there are a few key points to keep in mind:

1. You've got to know the organizational chart.
2. Not every title means the same thing in every organization.
3. Individuals with the titles don't always have the power.
4. There are always two types of organizations in every company: the published one and the political one.

Published vs. Political Organizational Charts

In every prospect's business, there will be the standard published organizational chart and the more important political one. A political organizational chart ranks the individuals in the company that have the ability to get things done.

Here's an example of the kind of information to use to create a political organizational chart: The President may have been with the company only three months, while the CIO has been with the company for twenty years

A Sample Organizational Chart

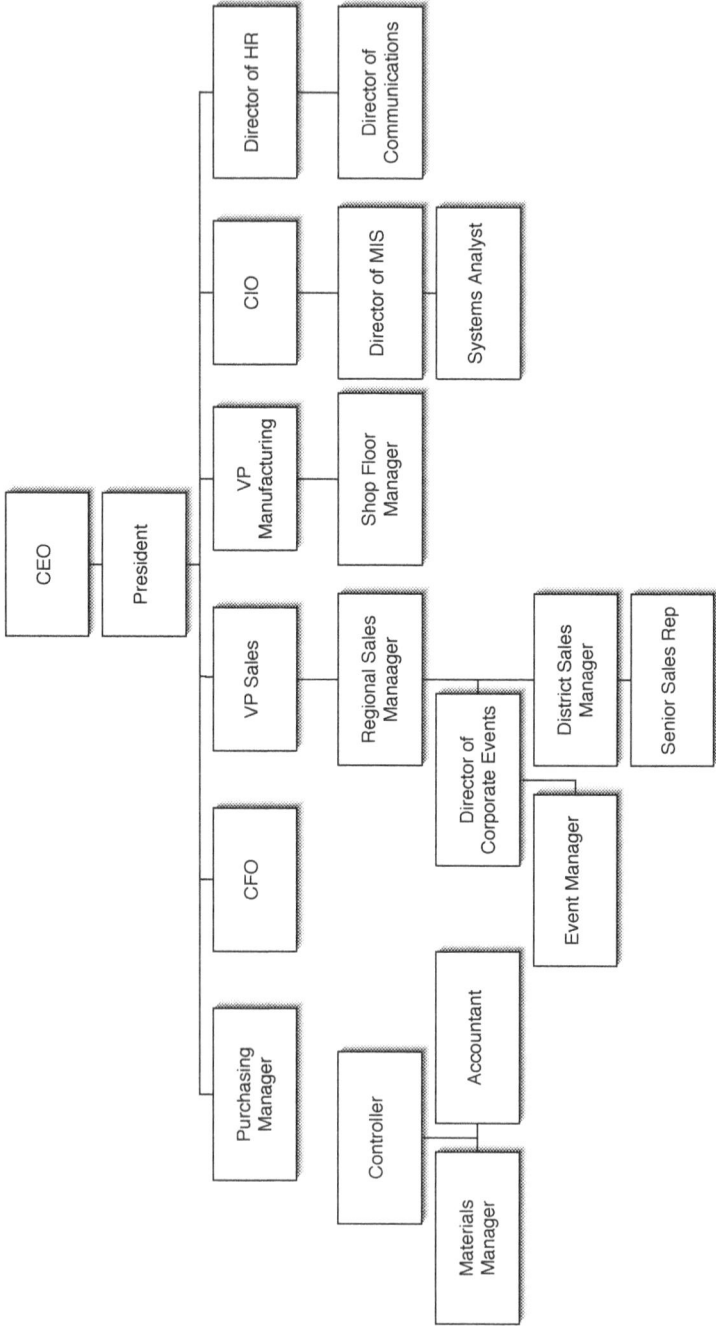

and is very close to the CEO. In this case, the CIO probably has more clout than the President, regardless of the difference in title.

You'll also need to locate any land mines in the political organizational chart. For example, it may be that if the CIO of a company endorses something, the VP of Marketing is going to fight it every time. In this situation, you'll have to work with each executive and get both on your team without being obvious about your strategy.

In selling, it's what you don't know that usually blows a deal apart. To be successful, you need to learn everything you can about all the relationships, issues, and politics within each company.

The following case study is the most extreme case of applying the Quid Pro Quo Selling approach I can imagine.

How to Level the Playing Field

I was an Executive VP for a small, self-funded software company. We were growing but had limited resources. I had the responsibility of setting guidelines for the sales force—the things we would and would not do in the course of pursuing business.

One day, a sales person called to let me know 3M was very interested in our solution. 3M was the 46th largest company in America at the time. Having them use our product would be a huge and highly marketable stamp of approval. This could bring millions to our bottom line, if they allowed us to use them as a reference.

3M needed sites for their 19 international branches. The sales rep wanted me to travel with him to their headquarters and give them a brief overview of our company's international strategy.

Considering we did not have an international strategy and did not have any installations outside North America, I was reluctant to waste my time on this call. To make matters worse, 3M had just signed a million-dollar agreement with a competitor for Enterprise Resource Planning (ERP) software. This competitor had worthy financial software that integrated perfectly to their ERP solution. This made me all but certain I was not interested in making the trip.

If you think there could be compelling reasons why someone should not buy your product, you are probably right. This is where direct questions helped me quickly determine if I had a chance or not. I decided to make 3M convince me they were seriously considering our solution. In this case, 3M had already purchased the competitor's ERP solution, so they had an established relationship with them.

The competitor provided service and operated offices in every country where 3M planned to install the software. In addition, the competition was a much larger organization. Given that our company had no international installations, no foreign offices, and no ERP solution, I would have bought from the competitor if I had been making the decision. I felt I was keeping the Quid Pro Quo selling dictum: Be honest with yourself at all times.

However, further qualification gave us some very useful information. 3M wanted to use the best software to meet their needs, and they wanted centralized support based out of Minneapolis. In that scenario, we could provide 3M with both the best software and customer support, all from Minnesota.

After much more qualification, and also some encouragement from our Founder/CEO, I decided to invest the time and make the trip. I flew off to make the sales call with our newly-minted international plan which would take an hour to present.

As it turned out, 3M was a good prospect, but our sales person had not done a particularly good job at qualifying. He didn't know the decision-maker, the time frame, the exact steps in the sales cycle, the specific evaluation criteria, or much else. I didn't let him come home on the plane either! He had to stay in Minnesota until he found an answer to every question that was unasked and unanswered about this opportunity. Never again would he make the mistake of not being prepared.

One of the things he discovered was that 3M was planning an international meeting in Singapore with the 19 executives who would be selecting the software solution. I received a call from the 3M project leader informing me of a meeting in Singapore in 10 days. Did I really want to go half way across the world for a three-hour presentation if there was only a slight chance 3M might buy from us?

At this point, I had never spoken with the decision-maker, and all the other competitive issues still lingered in my head. But our company would gain a great deal of status by signing 3M to 19 international sites, and my commission would be $150,000. So my response to the project leader was, "Maybe." In my mind, several conditions needed to be met. Remember—the prospect is not always right. My job is not to ask "How high?" when he asks me to jump. Setting expectations and establishing a respectful give-and-take relationship is the foundation of Quid Pro Quo selling. If I couldn't build such a relationship, I needed to move on to someone who was interested in solving a problem and not playing a sales evaluation game. I am not interested in wasting my time or theirs.

Believe me, this 3M project leader was quite put off by this approach. After all, from his point of view, 3M was offering me the opportunity of a lifetime. How dare I ask him a few hard, bold, direct questions!

I had definite reasons. I needed to understand why we'd get only three hours for our presentation. Also, I needed to know that I was on a level playing field with the competitor from whom they'd just purchased the ERP software. Singapore was a long ways away, but if I didn't go, my company was out of the evaluation. On the other hand, if I went to the expense of going, I wanted to make sure we had a legitimate chance.

The 3M project leader convinced me that my competitor and I were on a level playing field. He assured me both sides would get three hours and three hours only to make our presentations. At the end of this meeting, 3M would decide which package they thought would best serve their needs.

I wanted one more thing before I could commit to the trip. I needed to meet the decision-maker. Why? A project leader is not a salesperson and usually not the decision-maker. Don't make the mistake of letting your main contact do the selling for you. You need to give your pitch directly to the decision-maker. It's very important to stay in control of the sales process. If you turn the selling over to anyone else, you've lost control.

When I explained that I needed to meet with the decision-maker, the project leader told me that was impossible. I politely told him our company would not be traveling to Singapore. He explained that meant we were out of the deal. I told him understood and the conversation ended.

What it meant to me was no $150,000 commission check! It was a tough call, but if they wouldn't let me play my best hand, I was only wishing for a sale to close. Going to Singapore at that point would have been like entering a sailboat race for big money but without any sails. I could win only if all the other boats sank!

The next day I received another call from the project leader. He told me he had checked with the decision-maker (whom he refused to identify), and there was still no way he could meet with me. He went on to say the decision-maker met with all his people from the 19 foreign countries only once a year.

I didn't say a word to all this interesting but useless information. Finally when he stopped trying to sell me on why it was impossible to accommodate my request, he asked once more if I would come to Singapore.

In reality, nothing had changed. The project leader had thought through his sales strategy and once more had given me his pitch. I said, "No." My response made him absolutely crazy!

I proceeded to tell him again why I needed to meet with his boss. I asked, "Does he eat breakfast, lunch, and dinner?"

"Of course he does," the flustered project leader replied.

"If the guy won't sit down with me for 30 minutes and discuss the project and our solution after we do all you are asking for from me, then he won't buy from us," I said.

Again the project leader hung up, frustrated with my response. And again, I saw $150,000 slip right through my fingers. About an hour later, the project leader called me again. I answered the phone, and all he said was, "Okay!"

Playing dumb, I said, "Okay, what?"

"He'll meet with you." The decision-maker had agreed to meet with me for breakfast after our presentation. I pushed hard to speak with him before I went, but I couldn't make that happen. I flew off to Singapore, but I still had reservations.

These 3M guys had been in meetings since Sunday, trapped in the presentation room every day from 8:00 AM on. Our presentation was to be Thursday at 7 PM. This project leader wasn't helping us out much with that time slot! I gave my PowerPoint presentation, then sat in the back of the room and let the technical consultants show the software.

On the desk in front of me was the agenda for the week. I casually flipped through it and saw that my biggest fear had been realized. The competitor had the entire next day to present! We were not on a level playing field with our competitor. You can only imagine how frustrated I was, especially at myself. I knew better, and yet, there I was in Singapore, feeling like I had been nothing but a token comparison-offer with little real chance to earn the business.

Our presentation was excellent, and many of the CIOs came up afterwards and let us know how impressed they were with our solution.

At this point I felt I had nothing to lose. Our competitor had the entire day to present. 3M had already invested in their ERP solution. The project leader wasn't helping. And even though I knew we had the best solution, the cards were all stacked against us. The only good news for me was my breakfast the next morning with the decision-maker.

We all met for breakfast the next morning. The decision-maker was exactly what I expected—a gruff old guy who didn't want to be there and had no interest in

me. When I said "Good morning," he simply grunted.
We sat down at a very small table. One of the guys from
3M made the mistake of breaking the ice by asking,
"How do you think it went last night?" That was all I
needed to let loose.

"I'm glad you asked," I said. "I have to tell you I'm
disgusted by 3M and its representatives. I'm pretty sure
we don't want you as a customer. I know this is your
project leader's first conference, but you don't lie or treat
a potential partner the way he's treated us."

The project leader's face turned beet red as I
continued. Finally, the decision-maker had heard
enough. He put down his fork and said, "I am sorry you
had this experience. The feedback I got from your
presentation last night was exceptional. You solved a few
issues we've been trying to solve for years. Right now, I
would say you guys are way ahead. Perhaps you can do
one more thing for us. Could you go to Mexico next
month for one more presentation?"

My response was direct: "Absolutely not! We came
to Singapore on good faith and a promise of a level
playing field. We have spent a lot of time and money to

try and help you. You've seen enough information to make an informed decision. I know we can provide a solution that no one else can for you. We would love your business, but we were successful before we got here and will be successful when we leave."

The immediate outcome of this situation was that the project leader was taken off the project and sent to the Netherlands. 3M signed a multi-million dollar deal with us, with no discount! They gave us a great reference, a big press release, and put us in 19 countries.

Oh yeah, there was that $150,000 commission, too! My wife got that.

The point of this example? You've got to set the proper expectations right up front and truly believe you offer a better solution than the competitors if you want to really express yourself the way you need to in order to close business. In other words, your prospects have to be qualified and you have to maintain some level of control throughout the sales cycle.

CHAPTER TEN

Asking the Right Questions

You must define each company's needs to be able to give them the solution they need. To do this, ask the following kinds of questions.

1. Situation Questions

These are questions about the prospect's current situation which provide the background information necessary for you to discover potential problems. They are also used to warm up the prospect prior to delving into more sensitive problem areas.

Example: "At what point did you realize you had a need in this area?"

2. Problem Questions

These are questions about the prospect's problems, difficulties, or dissatisfaction with the existing situation. Problem questions are direct probes for needs.

Examples: "Is your current method of trading adequate?" or "Are you happy with the returns you are experiencing?"

3. Integration Questions

These are questions that expand a problem from the prospect's individual viewpoint to the viewpoints of others it might affect. They explore the effects of a problem on other people. Not only do these questions make the prospect more acutely aware of the problem and its effects but also they generate a sense of urgency. You only want to use these types of questions with prospects who are not opening up to you at all.

Example: "So who else does the growth or lack of growth in your business affect?"

4. Solution Questions

These are questions that help a prospect understand how he can solve his problems. The prospect will have to solve the problem. You can't solve it for him. Your job is to help him fully understand what information and tools he will need to solve the problem. Begin with an open-ended solution question.

Example: "So what would it take for you to be able to solve this problem?" If the prospect is unable to conceptualize the solution, use more specific questions: "If you could...would you...?"

5. Value Questions

With these questions, you're trying to lead the customer to tell you that he needs your product. If possible, he'll also understand the value (quantifiable or not) of the solution. When the prospect can visualize and verbalize the solution, a qualified need exists.

Example: "If you realized that our system does the research for you and gives you the answer to your problems, would you be interested?"

Facts vs. Feelings

Now that you have a qualified lead, it's time to ask different kinds of questions. These questions can be used in 1) filling the need, 2) moving toward commitment, and 3) cementing the sale.

Fact-finding questions provide you with valuable information to properly qualify your customer and to guide your direction. Feeling-finding questions enable you to learn about your customer's attitudes and opinions, and uncover fear, uncertainty, doubts, and buying motives.

Examples of Fact-Finding and Feeling-Finding Questions

Feeling-Finding	Fact-Finding
"How do you feel about..?"	"What difference would it make if…?"
"What do you think?"	"What?"
"Do you think it would be better if..?"	"Why?"
"What would you suggest?"	"When?"
"What is your opinion?"	"How?"
"Why is that important to you?"	"Where?"
"Why isn't that important to you?"	"Who?"
"What would be your reaction to..?"	"Why are you doing it like that..?"
"What would happen if..?"	"Could you give me an example of that?"
"What's your biggest concern?"	"Would it be fair to ask what you like most about…? least about…?"
"What do you think is a better way?"	
"Where do we start...?"	
"What do you think you need to do to achieve X?"	
"What do you think the real problem is?"	
"Could you tell me more about…?"	

Additional Qualifying Questions

The following are additional questions that can be used in qualifying. You will need to create a specific list that is unique to your product or company.

1. How did you find out about our company?

2. What prompted you to request information about our products?

3. How are you currently handling your needs (be specific)?

4. What has your experience been with the solution you mentioned?

5. Tell me about the type of things you envision that need to change?

6. What revenue growth are you achieving? What growth would you like to achieve?

7. How long have you been with this company?

8. What are the limitations of your current methods (prioritize)?

9. Would you consider another alterative now?

10. What would be the most important part of your evaluation?

11. How does your current situation affect you?

12. What are the limitations you see?

13. Who else is affected by these limitations?

14. What are you doing to resolve the issue?

15. (If you don't close on the first call): What is the time frame for your decision?

16. Who, other than yourself, will be involved in the decision?

17. Have you used technology to help you be more efficient in other areas of your life?

18. Do you believe our type of product can help you (be specific)?

SECTION THREE
Respect and the Sales Cycle

CHAPTER ELEVEN

Prospect Control

When you sell, who's in control? The old school teaches that the customer is always right. The customer is in control. If you suck up enough and lower your price enough, they'll eventually buy from you. The old school believes that the more services you offer a prospect, the better chance you'll have of winning the business.

Quid Pro Quo selling is totally the opposite to this type of approach. The prospect is not king. You are. You need to control all aspects of the sales cycle. Sales representatives who bend over backwards to please everyone soon weaken their spine.

There are two reasons why you should always be in control of the selling situation:

1. Your income depends on your sales volume.

2. You only have a limited amount of time to generate volume.

Let's look at the first reason. If you're like most salespeople, you earn a percentage of your income from commissions; in fact, many compensation plans are set up so that sales people earn at least 100% of their income from commissions. The sales volume you produce directly influences the amount you earn for the year. I'm always amazed at how many sales people seem to forget this fact. They seem to be content with letting the prospect control the selling situation. They seem to be content with earning far less than they should.

The second reason why you should control the selling situation is that you have a limited amount of time to sell each day, each week, and each year. Time is the most valuable asset you have as a salesperson. You don't have time to wish a prospect is going to buy from you. You don't have time to waste pursuing unqualified opportunities. You should structure your time so that its use benefits you and your goals the most.

One of the hard lessons I learned early in my sales career was that some companies employ what I'll call professional evaluators. These evaluators have nothing better to do than go to lunch with sales people, have meetings with sales people, and accept gifts from sales people. Unfortunately, they never buy. They are time eaters. They make you feel good about their intentions and usually express how much they like you, but they never can buy for one reason or another.

Those sales people who fall into the trap set by professional evaluators become unpaid tourists. They make trip after trip pursuing prospects, yet never bring home a signed agreement.

Once the prospect is helping you help him, it's important to remember that you're the one controlling the sales cycle. You set the ground rules.

··

THERE ARE SEVEN KEY STEPS IN THE PROCESS. THE PROSPECT

MUST AGREE TO:

1. LISTEN AND GRANT YOU ACCESS TO THE PEOPLE YOU NEED TO WORK

WITH.

2. EXPLAIN HIS SITUATION AND ISSUES.

3. DISCUSS HIS CONCERNS.

4. ACCEPT RESPONSIBILITY FOR HIS BUSINESS ISSUES.

5. DECIDE IF IT'S POSSIBLE TO SOLVE HIS PROBLEMS.

6. COMMIT TO CHANGE HIS HABITS.

7. AGREE TO A PLAN TO BUY.

You also want to set up realistic time frames for accomplishing these steps. Here are some guidelines. Work toward getting a commitment to steps 1, 2 and 3 during your initial conversation. The prospect must agree to these three steps before a qualified sales cycle exists.

Establishing a Quid Pro Quo relationship with the prospect should begin at first contact. There's no sense in sending literature to a prospect if he won't agree to a follow-up appointment, which will ensure that the literature has been read and the prospect is ready to discuss the merits of your product. If the prospect is vague and non-committal, then look for a better prospect.

By getting commitments from the prospect, you establish control and set the proper tone for the entire sales cycle. This also holds true for presentation timing. Don't agree to a presentation unless (a) a reasonable buy time frame has been established and (b) the decision maker is going to be involved.

I work with sales people daily who don't follow these two simple rules. Without exception, it comes back to bite them in the end. Either they have to do multiple presentations or their sales cycle suddenly stalls and they can't figure out why.

CHAPTER TWELVE

From First Call to Close

Prospective buyers typically evaluate three areas when making a decision: your company's reputation, technology/ease of use, and how your solution meets their needs.

Knowing this, when selling your products, you must be able to: develop your ability to present your company's and product's strengths, and differentiate it from the alternatives. This means that you have to know your company and your competition inside and out.

When selling the company's strengths, you reinforce its success by revealing the number of satisfied customers who are benefiting from your product. If presented correctly, your company's business philosophy, methods and track record versus its competitors' alternatives will be enough to win the business. Too many times, sales people don't put the required effort into this part of the sales cycle. If you've done this step properly, a demonstration is merely icing on the cake.

Most of my career has been spent in the software industry. In most cases, it's absolutely necessary to give the prospect a software demonstration. Prospects typically want you to prove to them that your product works. Most of the time, prospects don't have to ask for a demo because the sales people lean on the product in order to sell it.

In my experience, however, a short Power Point presentation should be enough to convince your prospects to buy if you: 1) ask a lot of good, open-ended questions, 2) resolve the prospect's issues, 3) paint a logical word picture, and 4) sell the strength of your company.

Understanding the Alternatives

In any marketplace, prospects commonly have multiple choices. It's easy for prospects to get confused. In many cases, this confusion leads to a sort of paralysis in which the prospect does nothing. You can get past this paralysis if you remember the words of Ben Feldman, the gentleman who sold more than a billion dollars worth of life insurance. In fact, he sold $15 million of new business in a single month at age 80! Mr. Feldman said, "You make a sale when the prospect understands that it will cost more to do nothing about the problem than to do something about it."

In order to get the prospect to understand Feldman's point, you must understand the prospect's problem and possible solutions, both yours and those of your competitors. You need to point out: 1) how your product will satisfy the prospect's needs, and 2) where the holes are in the competing strategies.

You must know what the alternatives are and why they are being considered. You should never disparage an alternative, especially not that of a worthy competitor. However, it's acceptable to point out differences between alternatives and what they will mean to your prospect. Prospects generally appreciate your helping them understand their options and clearing up their confusion between your solution and the alternatives.

Staying in Control

Too many times, salespeople pick up the phone and wing it. Winging it is an easy way to turn a sales opportunity into a mere price discussion. Trying to sell on price alone makes it much harder to overcome objections and far more difficult to close the sale.

When a sales person leads with the product in the sales cycle, 72% of the time they'll encounter pricing objections. Remember to put yourself in the prospect's shoes. Think through what the prospect's objections will be. Always acknowledge objections and address them immediately. Look for objections all the way through your sales cycle. Ask open-ended questions about the prospect's situation. Relate to them and steer them toward your company's product as the solution.

Qualifying and setting expectations are keys in controlling the sales cycle. Remember, the shorter the sales cycle, the more likely that it will be successful.

If I had not controlled the sales activity with Southwest Portland Cement and 3M, we would have had a much longer sales cycle, and we might not have won the business at all. The longer the sales cycle, the more opportunity there is for negatives to creep in and prevent your sale from happening. The customer may have a downturn in business. The decision-maker could leave the company. There are too many possibilities to list. Remember, in Quid Pro Quo selling, you have to establish a give-and-take relationship. To do so, you sometimes have to say, "I will, if you will." Sometimes you have to say, "No." It works, especially if you sound like a professional, prepare like a professional, and act like a professional.

Closing the Deal

If all the steps in the sales cycle are handled properly, the close should be a non-event. If you set the proper expectations, control the sales cycle, relate to the prospect as both a person and a professional, and you have created a give-and-take relationship, then closing the sale should be automatic. Your preparation, conviction, and true desire to offer a solution are the keys to closing the sale.

Selling is a natural chain of events. There should be no need for the such offers as the: 1) special-one-time discount 2) buy-now-before-the-price-goes-up, or any other worn-out ploys. You know them all, and so do your prospects.

Remember to play back their issues, remind them of why they were looking or why they need your product, reiterate the differences between the alternatives, and ask your prospects how they want to get started. If you've truly followed all the steps in the sales cycle, closing the deal is the easiest part of the job. (*See Appendix D: Checklist for Closing the Sale.*)

Selling vs. Telling

All sales people need to understand the difference between selling and telling. Selling is trying to make a valid point that will help win business and differentiate you from alternative options. Telling is giving information that may or may not be interesting and does not really serve a specific purpose. Selling works for you. Telling works against you.

When you're selling, stick to the issues and the easy-to-understand aspects of your product. You should spend 80% of your time bonding, setting expectations, qualifying, and painting logical word pictures. Spend only about 20% of the time demonstrating your product. The more complex your product, the more this rule applies. Remember, your objective is to sell, not teach.

When selling any product, application or system, it's important that you don't use a demonstration crutch to compensate for shortcomings in your sales skills. A demonstration crutch means leaning on your product too much to help you sell. Too often representatives want to show too much of their product, almost as though they're running a training class. More times than not, this approach confuses prospects and makes your product look harder to use than it really is.

If you find you're not achieving the results you should from your sales calls and presentations, telling could be the reason. Remember the saying, "Sell the sizzle, not the steak."

Ten Allowances of Sales

The words allowance, expectation, and empowerment can all be intertwined while employing the Quid Pro Quo selling approach.

....

10 KEYS TO BUILDING YOUR FRANCHISE:

1. YOU ARE ALLOWED TO DREAM.

2. YOU ARE ALLOWED TO BE CREATIVE.

3. YOU ARE ALLOWED NOT TO KNOW ALL THE ANSWERS.

4. YOU ARE ALLOWED TO ASK QUESTIONS.

5. YOU ARE ALLOWED TO MAKE MISTAKES

6. YOU ARE ALLOWED TO PUSH BACK AND SAY, "NO."

7. You are allowed to act as though you work for yourself.

8. You are allowed to control all the selling activity.

9. You are allowed to try a new approach.

10. You are allowed to create a respectful give-and-take relationship with your prospects.

You matter. Your prospect matters. So does dignity and a little thing called dreaming. Think big. That's part of the magic of selling and being successful.

CHAPTER THIRTEEN

Dynamics of the Sales Cycle

So far we've looked at the role of sales people and how to develop goals. In addition, we've discussed the sales cycle: process, prospecting, qualification, and selling on a personal level. The next step is to understand the dynamics of the sales cycle in a structured methodology.

A sales cycle consists of the steps you must follow in order to close a sale. The sales cycle has three phases. You can work through these phases very quickly, sometimes in just one call.

The three phases of the sales cycle:

1. Needs what?
2. Details how?
3. Risk why?

At this point we're going to look at the sales cycle in even more detail. Remember, it will vary depending on your product and market.

Phase I: Needs what?

In the first part of the sales cycle, you must determine if the prospect has a need that can be satisfied by your product or service.

After you have identified the key players and have had them agree to a plan, then you have a qualified prospect.

Notice the words "have them agree to a plan." This is much different then the prospect just telling you what they want from you and you agreeing to step and fetch. The foundation of the Quid Pro Quo sales approach is about creating a working relationship and situation that is good for everyone involved. Any prospect dictating the terms of an evaluation is never going to be good for the sales person.

The other aspect of Phase I is uncovering the pending event. A pending event is the event or issues driving the need for your product or services. Either the prospect will have already identified a pending event or you will have to create one for them. It is almost impossible to sell anything at any time if there is not a pressing need. Some examples of prospects pending events might be: 1) Plans to attend an upcoming trade show and so they need marketing literature printed before that date. 2) Have to be off the shared server by a certain date and thus need to buy a new CPU before that date. 3) Budget dollars will be lost if money is not spent by year's end.

There is an endless list of potential pending events. The point here is to uncover the issue by asking enough good questions of the right person.

Finally, I have found the best questions to identify a specific, motivating pending event is to ask the prospect: "Why didn't you pursue this six months ago? What will be the consequence if you are in the same position six months from now?" These questions will usually flush out the pending event if one exists.

If one is not obvious or you are unable to flush one out, then you must try to create a pending event. Creating fear, uncertainly and doubt in the prospects mind, better known as FUD, is the best way do this. To do this effectively, you must first have a clear understanding of the issue, how it is affecting the business and the effect it will have on the person you are selling to personally. You have to understand how this person is judged to be really effective at creating FUD. Please don't ever try to create FUD by using the "fire sale" approach.

"We only have a few left so you better buy now" or worse, "the price is going up at the of the month." Even the most novice buyers understand these are usually just sales tactics. Here's an example of creating a pending event: "To deliver by the day you want, you'll need to get your order in by the 31st or the marketing VP will not have the literature they need at the show in time."

Again, there are many forms and examples of creating pending events. Take a minute and write down four to five versions of real pending events that might be applicable to what you are currently selling.

Phase II: Details how?

People Surveys: Your goal is to understand each prospect as a person, and to identify his or her buying motives. The following will help you:

Identify the prospect's attention span. Determine if the prospect is driven by:

technology
security needs
recognition factors
the size of his bank account
his spare-time activities
pride

During Phase II, determine the prospect's ability to absorb information. Understand your prospect. Then plan and influence using compatible behavior. And watch out for anything that is out of character.

Functional Surveys—A functional survey is part of the qualification process. Only by thoroughly understanding your prospect's issues can you determine if you can provide a solution to their problems. A functional survey should always be your road map through the sales cycle. Here are some typical questions you'll have to answer:

Have they identified their problem(s)?

Have they quantified the cost?

How long have they had the problem(s)?

Is there a solution you can provide?

Do you have full knowledge of the situation?

Does your prospect think he can solve the issue with a different alternative?

Many times people tell me selling is about relationships, but when I ask them how much they really know about their prospects on the personal side they usually go blank. There are many examples of understanding prospects at the personal level, especially early in the sales cycle, that will help you relate to them better and for them to understand you are sincerely looking out for their best interest. The best way to uncover the personal side of a prospect is to ask appropriate personal questions. It is interesting that you can ask people almost anything and they will answer you. If you challenge this notion, next time you are on an airplane sitting next to a stranger, strike up a conversation. Soon you can ask them almost anything and they will tell you. In the context of your business relationship, you can also ask almost anything.

The first time you ask a personal question, they will usually give a business reply. They are not accustomed to salespeople expressing concern about them on an individual level so they answer behind their business wall. What you have to do at that point is explain you understand the business aspects. What you are asking is about them personally.

As an example, a conversation might go something like: "Jean, VP of Sales, thus far you have told me your forecasts are inaccurate, your revenues are off, and you having a lot of sales turn over. How is that effecting you personally?"

The honest answer would likely be, "I'm losing sleep at night; I might get fired if this situation doesn't change; and I am losing credibility with the President."

Another example: "Because it takes three weeks to close your books, what affect is that having on you from a personal standpoint?"

I actually had a CFO tell me that he had to work a lot of weekends and it was really starting to affect his marriage.

Of course with this kind of information it is easy to understand how you can impact the prospect in a positive way and build a lasting relationship once you help them clear up the personal issues.

Correct the thinking or perception that business is business and personal is personal. To most people their careers and jobs are very personal. Where do most people spend their time outside of their home? At work! It's all personal! It's key for the successful sales person to understand the personal effects of each issue on every person they are dealing with inside of a prospect's organization.

Presentations

We discuss the rules for presentation management in detail later in the book. But at this point, I'd like to explain when and how to use your presentation. Too many times sales people use this step incorrectly. The anxious sales person will push for a presentation as early as possible in the sales cycle, hoping to create enough interest to move forward. This belief is a product of the old conventional wisdom, and it's wrong.

You shouldn't use your presentation to catch your prospect's attention and generate early interest. The presentation should be used as a confirmation step after your prospect has learned enough about your product or service that he's ready to make the buying decision.

In most cases, prior to your presentation, you'll want the prospect to visit your web site, review collateral materials, undergo a pricing discussion, talk to some references, and agree on steps to be followed if the presentation meets his expectations. It's too costly in time and money to give unqualified presentations, hoping they'll work magic.

Customer visits and reference calls are a common part of most sales cycles. Avoid giving control of the activity to your prospect. Most salespeople will give a prospect three to four references upon request. Typically, the prospect doesn't call references as quickly as you'd like, and the sales cycle is stalled until he gets through this step. You must stay involved and never give the prospect the opportunity to delay the sales cycle. In addition, you may not know what your reference will say. To stay in control, touch base with your references before you give them out to make sure they are still willing to speak on your behalf and to coach them on what to say.

Here's the best way to do it. When a prospect asks for references, gladly oblige her, with the condition that you set up the call. A method that always works is to tell the prospect that it's your company's policy to respect the time of its customers and that you will respect your prospect's time in the same way once she becomes your customer.

The same theory holds true for a customer site visit. Don't ever let your prospect visit a customer unless you accompany them. This is key, and it's irresponsible on your part if you ever let this happen.

Cost Justification

Unfortunately, not every product or service can be hard-dollar-cost justified. The good news is, most products and services can have some formula attached to them to make it easier for prospects to see value and buy your offerings. You should always make your product or service as hard-dollar-cost justified as possible.

Phase III: Risk Why?

This is the last part of the sales cycle. Work hard to take the risk out of buying what you are selling. The prospect needs the comfort of knowing he's making the right decision. You must make it very clear that your product or service provides the solution he's looking for and that the actual risk comes if he doesn't buy your product or service.

Most of us experience some level of buyer's remorse regardless of what we buy. The bigger the purchase, the more buyer remorse we experience. Heck, I get buyer's remorse. I'm always wondering, "Was there a better deal somewhere; was this the best I could have done; did I really need this?" Most people in decision-making positions have an emotional attachment to the buying decisions they make.

Recently a couple of senior Executives from *Selling Power Magazine* made a call on me. Of course I'm familiar with this magazine, and their readership is getting close to 500,000 sales professionals. They were extremely intrigued with our new product called Executive Link. It is the first product of its kind to help sales people relate to the decision-makers at their level, talk the talk so to speak. They were going to do an editorial piece on Executive Link for their readers. Our course this was very exciting news for all of us at Sales Builders. They went further and suggested we buy advertising in the magazine, as well. Full-page color ads in major magazines are not cheap to say the least. I had never done a campaign like they suggested.

The potential was undisputable, but putting a lot of money out with no guaranteed results was a huge risk in my mind. The executives from the magazine understood my concerns. They acknowledged my concerns, and appreciated the amount of the investment as being significant.

They were also very good at selling. They had worked in similar situations and showed me ads and, most impressively, the resulting testimonials. They had statistic after statistic. They explained the demographics of their readers. They continued to share genuine enthusiasm for our new product. They were doing everything in reason to take the risk out of making a buying decision for me. They also realized what I was really looking for was not an ad campaign but a long-term partnership.

Again they had everything in their hip pocket I needed. They took the risk out of the buying equation for me as much as they could. I went ahead and bought in to their program, and it was a huge success. It would have been a more costly decision to not do anything. We have gained many new clients from our work with *Selling Power Magazine.*

If you've handled all the previous steps correctly, the price negotiations and scheduling resources should be an easy process and, the result, a signed agreement.

CASE STUDY

The Indigo Company

Recently, I worked with Indigo, a company that sold investment software via the telephone and in seminars. It's a technical-analysis-based trading system that enables investors to determine which stocks to buy and which trading strategy would enable them to achieve specific returns. Considering that most people don't have a strategy or a disciplined plan they follow when it comes to investing in the stock market, this software is revolutionary.

My job was to help educate the sales force on how
to effectively sell its system. As is the case with many
start-ups, the product was so good the company initially
got away with not following good sales procedures and/
or hiring less experienced sales people. However, at some
point, even companies with great products must face
competition or a market downturn, and it was critical that
this company's sales force be trained to fight off those
forces that threatened their continued growth.

One day I walked into one of Indigo's sales offices
in southern California to work with a team to sharpen
their selling skills. Obviously, I wanted to help them
learn the fundamentals of Quid Pro Quo selling.

I roamed around the office and met everyone. I
listened and observed how they dealt with their
prospects. These guys had limited sales experience and
training. A few had a day or two of formal sales training.
Most had no prior sales training at all.

They were cold calling prospects and leaving
messages like: "Mr. Jones, our clients are making a lot of
money over here at Indigo. If you're serious about
making money, please hurry and call me back!"

I also heard a sales rep say: "This could be one of your last chances to take advantage of our March special. We can save you a lot of money, but you need to call me back today."

These messages sounded similar to those used by a car sales pitchman on a television commercial at 1:00 am. The type of messages and sales approaches used by Indigo's sales people generated a similarly negative response.

This great group of salesmen, however, was hungry to learn and succeed. When I brought the group together, I told them that the first step to be successful is to be honest with themselves and the people they were trying to help.

Next, I asked the very simple question, "Would you buy from yourself? If you received a message like the ones you are leaving, would you call the person back?" Without hesitation they all said, "No."

"If you wouldn't respond to yourself," I asked, "why would you expect a prospect to?" The truth is, prospects subjected to such selling methods will stay as far away from you as possible unless they have an overwhelming need for your solution or unless your product sells itself. After a little self-examination, these sales reps completely changed their approach. The results were dramatic.

CHAPTER FOURTEEN

Responding to Objections

Michael Jordan said, "Obstacles don't have to stop you. If you run into a wall, don't turn around and give up. Figure out how to climb it, go through it or around it."

Every prospect will have objections, regardless of your product or solution. To respond effectively, you need to prepare a list of every objection your prospect might have. Be prepared with a response. Keep asking questions to find out what the prospect's real issues are. Find out if it is really an issue or if, in fact, he's testing you. Find out if he's just trying to put you off as a means of avoiding a decision.

If you are absolutely certain your prospect will have an objection over a few issues, be proactive and put those issues on the table. Address them immediately so you can move on and secure your sale.

You have to really listen and determine if the objection your prospect is putting forth is a legitimate issue or if he is just trying to avoid something else. The following picture portrays an objection that is not legitimate. A woodsman chopping down a tree with an ax claims he doesn't have time to talk to the salesperson about buying a chain saw. Obviously, using an ax is much harder, slower, and less efficient than using a chain saw. Still, the woodsman has no time for the chain saw salesperson.

A caption to this picture could say many things. The one I like best is one I've heard a million times from prospects: "I'll think about it." Think about it? Is a tree going to have to fall on this guy's head before he can make a decision? There's no decision to make. A visual aid like this one can get a prospect laughing about his indecision and is generally an effective tool for the salesperson.

A similar illustration shows a salesperson trying to sell machine guns to a knight with a sword and shield who is trying to fight off an army. The caption on that one reads, "Sorry, no time right now." When you run into this type of objection, tackle it head on. Don't be shy. Use solid logic, reasoning skills and word pictures to overcome delay tactics by prospects.

Following are some typical objections and how to overcome them.

Objection	Reason for Objection	How to Overcome
Want a 30-day trial	Other companies offer this	Won't do product justice without training or commitment on the prospect's part.
Product looks difficult	Novice prospect	Product is very user friendly. Comes with training and customer support.
Price is too high	Other products cost less	Show historical performance.
I don't have enough $	May not understand the value	Point out how their current situation is costing them money.
I need to research	Didn't get this in your pitch	Take them to your web site. Sell them again on your company's attributes.
I'll look it over and call	Confused–doesn't understand	Go over performance in detail.
Going on vacation	Stalling	Revisit need and or pending event.
I want a guarantee	Numbers they have seen are too high	Stress unlimited support. Ask what other products were guaranteed? We can't either and explain.

| What if I want to return it? | Scared or tire kicker (not serious) | You are exposed to our proprietary information. |
| I don't have time right now | Doesn't understand value | Demo or schedule a demo. Ask how much time their present situation is taking. Their most valuable asset is their time. How are they spending it trying to make more money? |

Many objections will come up in the course of a sales cycle. Some are based on real concerns and others are merely tests of your conviction and understanding of the issues. You have to know the difference between the two. In either case, you need to prepare and anticipate the objections your prospect will throw at you.

If you have been selling the same solution for a while, you've probably encountered most objections. In some cases, it's appropriate to bring up the objections before your prospect does. I'd caution you on doing this, because, if not executed properly, you can come across very much like a quota-carrying salesperson. The only time it's really acceptable to do this is when you're certain the prospect will bring up the objection once he's had a chance to think through the situation. By preempting him, you gain credibility and shorten your sales cycle.

CHAPTER FIFTEEN

Defensible Pricing

Identifying a product or service pricing strategy is always intriguing. With some organizations, price is based on what the market will bear. With others, price is based on a return on investment (ROI) calculation. Some companies merely toss a dart at the board. In truth, price should be based on the value of the product you bring to your customer. As a sales person, you should know how your product's price was determined.

Once you understand your product's pricing, you can articulate and sell the value more aggressively. Ninety-three percent of all salespeople offer a discount before being asked! Why? Because most representatives believe that lowering price will help close the sale. Sometimes this is true, but, more often prospects view your lowering the price as a red flag.

Offering a price discount before it's asked for creates problems.

The discounted price you offer becomes the new starting point for negotiations. Once you've offered a discount, it's almost impossible to get the price back up.

For instance, you've just finished selling the prospect on how outstanding your product is. Lowering price reduces your credibility, as well as the value of your product or service.

Think about it. Your prospect has just heard all your company's attributes, the benefits of your product, how much better it is than any alternative, and that she absolutely must have it. Now, the first thing you do is offer a discount? What kind of signal are you sending?

If you follow the fundamentals of Quid Pro Quo selling, you'll be able to receive the full value for your product. Successful qualifying includes establishing your price early in the sales cycle and understanding the buyer's price expectations. Get rid of the question, "What's your budget?" This is a question that launches the sales security system. There are many other ways to ask the same question. My favorite is, "What do you expect to spend to solve this problem?" It gives you the same information without putting the prospect on the defensive.

The next story illustrates how I established my price in a real-world situation.

CASE STUDY

Interfacing with Georgia-Pacific

I was selling to Georgia Pacific (GP), a Fortune 50 Company, based in Atlanta. Georgia Pacific is one of the largest suppliers of paper products in the world. Like most large organizations, they are used to dictating the terms and price for everything they buy. Smaller companies typically think that having large, prestigious companies use their products gives their product instant credibility. It's natural for large companies to exploit this type of thinking to get deep discounts in price.

I sold financial application/accounting software, and, as with most good software packages, our company had developed a graphical user interface (GUI) to go in front of the accounting software. The GUI gave the software the Windows® look and created ease of use.

We didn't sell the GUI as a separate product, but GP wanted to buy it. In the middle of our financial software applications presentation, they asked the founder of our company what it would cost for them to purchase the GUI. I was totally surprised when the founder replied, "You'll have to work that out with Bob."

I quickly went into my questioning mode. "How much do you feel it would cost you to develop something like this?" "Is time an issue for you?" "What are your alternatives?" I asked a few more questions, but GP wasn't giving me helpful information.

Though panicked, I collected myself and said, "The GUI will cost $700,000."

GP's representatives said the price was too high, and the presentation continued. (By the way, all large companies will always tell you your price is too high. I could have said, "$10" and I would have likely gotten the same response.)

After the presentation, GP showed their hand a bit and continued to express interest in the GUI. They let me know it wasn't in their budget, but they liked the product. They started to sell me on why it would be good for our company to let them have it for free. But there was no way that would happen. We really weren't looking to sell it at any price.

I told GP that we were definitely not going to give away GUI and proposed that we talk again if they found some money in their budget. They said they'd look into their budget situation, and they still wanted to evaluate the GUI.

Their research teams looked at the product for weeks, which did not require much, if any, of my time. They decided they wanted to use our GUI for software applications they would develop in house.

The CIO and Georgia Pacific's corporate attorney invited me to a meeting to discuss how they could acquire this product. Having been involved with a few of these meetings in the past, I had a pretty good idea what to expect. But this time they really caught me off guard.

The three of us met in their palatial offices. In a company like GP, the CIO has a lot of decision-making power, deals with multi-million-dollar budgets, and is usually inaccessible to outside sales people. Without exception, CIOs expect to get their way. As I sat down, the CIO said, "Like I told you a few months ago, we don't have any money budgeted for this product, so we need you to give it to us for free." Not realizing it, I made the mistake of rolling my eyes at his statement.

"Who do you think you are?" the CIO screamed. "I told you, we have no budget for this! We can give you more business than your company can imagine, and I don't need your attitude." (This was an interesting way to learn that I do tend to roll my eyes at things I think are ridiculous.)

At this point, I hadn't said a single word in the meeting. After the CIO finished trying to intimidate me, I looked him right in the eyes and said, "I'm sorry you feel that way, and I meant no disrespect with the facial expression I made, but I told you the price months ago. I also told you we were not going to give the product away. So this meeting is over. Please call me when you get some funds." I closed my notebook and stood up.

My response shocked him as much as his outburst shocked me. He asked me to stay and see if we could work it out. The end result was that Georgia Pacific paid $700,000 for the product and received no discount.

By setting the expectation right up front, I earned the right to tell him my firm price.

The only time to give a discount is when you get something back from the prospect. If you don't, you're signaling to the prospect that it's acceptable for him to control the sale. Instead, you might say, "I'll lower my price in exchange for three qualified leads and referrals from your personal network." When you do this, the prospect feels he's getting a deal because he's helping you. In addition, you've saved face with the prospect by getting something in return for your discount. You haven't devalued your product, and the prospect gets a lower price. Everyone wins in this situation.

CHAPTER SIXTEEN

Steps for a Successful Presentation

Assuming you've successfully followed the Quid Pro Quo methodology through the other stages of the sales cycle, your presentation can be the most important step in closing your prospect. It's essential that your presentation focuses on your prospect's issues. Once you've found a qualified prospect, you absolutely must:

Know enough about your product and their current issues to give them all the information necessary to make a good decision.

Draw pictures to illustrate points and benefits. A picture paints a thousand words.

Develop a rapport that makes them feel that you have a genuine concern for their situation.

Be positive, dynamic, and polished.

Sell the company effectively.

Know the prospect's requirements. Present the appropriate aspects of your product.

Touch on all their hot points.

Nine Steps to a Successful Presentation

1. Meeting: Having a conference call with everyone that will be involved in the presentation is very beneficial. I understand that this can be

challenging to achieve. The objective is to help you determine what information is required prior to the presentation.

2. Agenda: Before the start of every presentation, it is required that you set the agenda for the topics you plan to discuss. Before you start, let everyone in attendance add to your agenda to ensure you are meeting every specific need. This professional preparation sets you apart from normal canned-style presentations.

3. Customizing Data: This is a very effective step to take if at all possible. Address the prospects' particular regional issues, talk about the type of methods your prospects are accustomed to, and develop easy-to-understand models/examples to walk through with them. All of these can definitely be winners.

4. Listing the Issues: A flip chart or board for listing all issues should be available. These issues include all of the requirements that were given during the presentation. This is your presentation guide, and it keeps you and the prospect on track.

5. Selling the Company: Remember that the prospects' knowledge of your company and how your product meets the prospects' specific requirements is the key to getting the sale. Selling your company and differentiating your product from the alternatives is the first step. I am a strong believer that a Power Point presentation is the best way to achieve this.

6. Chalk Talk: Prior to starting a formal presentation, you should address how your product can resolve each issue on the list. Doing this effectively can initiate questions from your prospects, which can pinpoint the prospect's main area of concern. Using this information, you can customize your presentation and shorten it, which will keep the prospects' attention focused. Also, a good chalk talk can get the prospects "into" your presentation prior to its start, enabling them to sit back and enjoy the rest.

7. Demonstration: If possible, always demonstrate what you've successfully accomplished for customers in the past or could do for the prospect in the future. Talk in terms of features, benefits, and differences from your competitors' solutions. Go down the list of issues, showing as little or as much detail as the particular issue warrants. Remember, you are selling, not teaching or telling. Your objective is to get signed orders when you are finished with your web cast, dinner meeting, or seminar.

8. Confirmation: When the presentation is finished and all the questions have been answered, once again go over the list of issues. Get confirmation that the prospects have a clear understanding of how your solution meets their particular requirements. This is important because after a presentation, things can get a bit fuzzy. Also, if there are any misconceptions about your presentation, this is the time to get rid of them.

9. Close: Statistics show the most common problem sales people have is the ability to close. To be a successful closer, you must know how your product meets the prospects' requirements, and, more importantly, the prospects must know how your product meets their requirements. If you communicate this information effectively, you should get a commitment to buy.

There are all types of ways to close. The best close is simple: Ask for the order. You'll never get an order if you don't ask for it. If there is an objection, try to overcome it and ask again. You may have to ask repeatedly. Don't be afraid that you'll hurt someone's feelings by asking for an order.

There is no sense losing a sale when a couple of direct questions will indicate the next step you need to take or uncover an objection that hasn't been addressed.

Follow up

It's important for sales people to keep in touch with their prospects after the presentation. You may have given a great presentation, but if you let time lapse and your prospects are exposed to other alternatives, he could very well become confused. If you haven't been able to close your prospects within five days of your presentation, you have likely lost the opportunity.

Comfort that Closes the Sale

Many times prospects will want to check references, visit other customers, and receive a written proposal from you.

References: It's not unusual for a prospect to want to speak to someone else you have done business with prior to making her final decision. Such a conversation generally gives her the comfort she needs before committing to your product. It's not that the prospect doesn't believe what you've told her in your presentation, but quite often she needs this affirmation by an outside source to cement her decision. Part of the Quid Pro Quo methodology expects you to always remain in control of every selling opportunity. Once you hand over a prospect to anyone else, you've lost control.

Customer Visits: These can be powerful closing tools. If you have a customer who had issues similar to those of your prospect and whom you've successfully helped, sometimes a customer visit is all you will need to close a sale. Remember, you must have absolute control if you choose to take this step. Leave nothing to chance. When selling, always assume Murphy's Law is in effect, "Anything that can go wrong, will go wrong."

If a site visit is required, then make sure you are present. Always coach your customer on what you would like him to say to your prospect. Always create an agenda for your visit, and have it reviewed and agreed to by all parties involved before the visit.

Proposal: Proposals can be a very effective sales tool. Was your last proposal a "silent salesperson" or just structured numbers on a page? Every opportunity you have to show your understanding of a prospect's business problems, along with your unique solution, is an opportunity to sell. The proposal is a great opportunity. The proposal also lets you create a pending event with the goal of moving your prospect to action. Every proposal should have an expiration date with the implication that the prices or terms will change if a decision is not made within a given period of time.

If everything else goes correctly, you finally get to the point where the prospect says he'd like to buy your product or service. At this point, you've won. You've been selected. However, the sales process is not over. You've still got to negotiate the agreement. This has to be done carefully, as seemingly small points can turn into big problems.

Knowing When to Budge in Contract Negotiations

During negotiations, both parties must reach an agreement on price, terms, resource commitments, and time frames. You should always have a clear understanding of why you were selected by the prospect before you negotiate. If the reasons are significantly compelling, there is no reason to negotiate. Stick to your prices and terms.

Let's assume you have executed the steps in the Quid Pro Quo approach. To be honorable and save face you must:

1. Never give something away without getting something back.

2. Remind the prospect that early in the sales cycle you told him what you would and would not do to earn his business. (Read the Georgia Pacific story again).

3. The buyer needs to feel good about the process.

4. You have to meet the prospect's expectations.

5. You, as the sales person, must have the belief and conviction that you can bring a solution to your potential buyer.

Interestingly, when you stick with your original price, prospects usually feel better about their buying decisions. Cutting your price often diminishes the value of your product in the prospects' eyes. Don't give the prospect cause to wonder. If your product is so good, why discount it?

Buyer's Remorse: The Next Day Call

Everyone has buyer's remorse. Remove the balance of any doubt by reassuring and talking in terms of a promising future. I belong in the Buyer's Remorse Hall of Fame. For example, when I buy a simple item of clothing, I'm telling myself that I didn't really need it before I leave the store.

The positive emotions of buying peak at the time of purchase. As soon as most people sign the check, their excitement has started to dissipate. The good news is that their enthusiasm generally returns once they're reminded of the benefits they receive because they bought the product.

Your biggest concern is the period of time when your customer is sorry that he bought. A call from you the next day with some reassurance will go a long way toward building customer loyalty and will make your new customer feel secure that he made a good decision. Remember, regardless of your business, you'll need references and referrals. Keep your customer's positive vision alive after the sale with a call.

CHAPTER SEVENTEEN

Mutual Respect at the Top

I would be remiss if we didn't review applying the Quid Pro Quo selling approach at the top. You could read this book, digest every word in it, and execute each aspect of what it offers you. But if you apply or execute your newfound skills to the wrong person in the organization, you are likely to fall short of selling anything.

As mentioned earlier, the world we live in has changed in recent years. The events of 9/11 have had effects in many different ways. The way business is done has changed over the past several years. The market is more competitive than ever. Information and knowledge is being transferred at rates never seen before. Buyers are more educated and demand more from their suppliers and sales people. It goes without saying that in today's market, decision makers expect sales people to know their offerings. More importantly, they demand that your sellers understand their business as well. To become the coveted "Trusted Advisor," sellers must be able to not only understand the executives' business, but must also be able to relate to them on a personal basis. If they are unable to do so, then they will be perceived as just another quota carrying salesperson with the only objective being to sell them something.

Regardless of the industry, the market is tight. Organizations are under pressure for results. More importantly, decision makers are being held accountable for their decisions and the results they achieve. Sales people face a new competitor in the market like never before called "Status Quo." At the same time, the emergence of the internet has shifted more power to the buyer. In the current market environment, the ability to sell business solutions rather than products or services is essential and can only be done at the executive level.

Understanding the unique business and personal challenges of selling to executives is crucial to success. Executives today are people who have little time or patience for quota carrying sales people. They are working longer hours, answering to more people, and have little time on their hands. Salespeople need to establish credibility early in the sales cycle, both for themselves and for their company. How can they make the most of such limited time to establish trust and gain continued access to the executives? "Trusted Advisor" status! Many sales organizations today boast that they have a consultative sales approach. What this implies is that their salespeople form a consultant-type relationship with the decision makers in the organizations they are selling to.

Executives buy because they feel understood, not because they understand! Understanding this statement is essential. We are all classically trained to present, show, tell, and explain in pain staking details all about what we have to offer. The bad news is once in awhile it works.

Where does this overwhelming compulsion to get them to understand come from? Most likely it has come from the training you have been given internally. Most organizations hire new sales people, give them a quick company orientation. Most of the time in this orientation is spent on features and functions of the products or services. They might even spend time on the competitive difference you will enjoy while you are out in the market place selling. Think back. How much time is ever spent talking about the people you should be selling to?

However, if you can gain knowledge of each person you approach in the sales cycle and truly relate to them on their level, you will have a completely different dynamic. This is true professional selling; it is the difference in winning or losing. It's also another reason why it is so important to establish a relationship of mutual respect early in the sales cycle.

I'm have been asked for years, "Where can I get this knowledge to be able to relate to executives?"

How to Determine Who is the Final Decision Maker

Step 1

Ask your manager (Obvious, but often forgotten)
Review past agreements to see who signed them
Ask other successful sales people
Ask the prospect

Step 2

Find information on relating to executives.
Search the web site for personal data
Read the annual report
Read recent news releases; look for quotes
Ask other in the prospect's organization about executives
Befriend the gate keeper

Step 3

Become a Trusted Advisor. You might not have ever been a CFO, CEO, or VP, but you have to put yourself in their shoes and relate to them at their level. There are several way to gather this knowledge to give you confidence, credibility, and the courage to sell with mutual respect at the top.

Interview executives in your own company that hold the role
Ask friends who might have this role
Network with people who might know someone in this role that can introduce you; interview them
Research with Executive Link. Executive Link is a unique tool that links sales professionals to executive's roles, and details the issues they face, others that are affected by these issues, industry trends, industry terms, and solution to the issues. This product also provides the ability to customize the solutions to your products or services.

You can link your case studies, competitive information, and past proposals to the Executive Link system to maximize the effectiveness. Executive Link is the only product I know of designed to help sales professionals not only create the perception of a "Trusted Advisor," but actually become one. More info can be found at www.executivelink.com.

One of the leading factors considered by sales managers we have surveyed and who have successfully improved sales results in 2003 compared to 2002, was their teams ability to effectively sell at executive levels.

In many surveys taken from both executives and sales people in recent years, most sellers are not perceived as business consultants. There are various reasons for this. The overwhelming reason is that most sellers do not take the actions laid out in this book. Instead they recite the company's marketing literature in hopes it will resonate with the buyer.

Sales people have been taught over the years to sell features and benefits. As the years evolved, this was extended to sell features, benefits, and solutions. The best salespeople took this one step further and sold features, benefits, solutions—and were able to differentiate their solutions from alternatives that were available to decision makers. In the current market place, sellers have to do better and evolve once again.

Sellers need to be able to relate their solution to the specific issues that are keeping the executives or decision makers awake at night. They have to be able to offer them insight, knowledge, and solutions that will make their lives better from both a business and a personal standpoint. Many sellers realize that good selling is about building good relationships with buyers. Yet they forget that business issues transcend the office and affects buyers in a very personal way. It is of the utmost importance to be able to understand how specific business issues are affecting executives at home and relate to them on that level. We will examine questions that all sellers should be asking themselves in every sales opportunity they pursue.

"No Decision" and Forecast Accuracy

Statistics show that 40% of salespeople face such bouts of *call reluctance* at some point that it costs them their jobs. Additionally, my research has found that if we added one word in front of *call reluctance*, executive, or *executive call reluctance*, this percentage would at least double.

80% of sales people sell at the wrong level

This is a staggering percentage, but nevertheless it is true, especially early in the sales cycle. Too many sellers have the feeling that they have to earn their way up in the organization before they can call on the executives.

This is a costly error in judgment. Sales people typically spend their time with "influencers" or "recommendors" vs. decision makers. What is lost on most sellers is that if these "influencers" or "recommendors" were good at selling, they probably would have pursued this career vs. the roles they are in now.

The most important part of a sales cycle is the ability to qualify the prospect. If a salesperson is qualifying the wrong person at the wrong level, the entire qualification process becomes suspect. It is evident that sellers are too low in the organization by the issues the Sales VP faces day in and day out. The Sales VP is constantly facing issues of forecasting accuracy.

THERE ARE THREE MAIN ISSUES WITH FORECASTING THAT

NEED TO BE CLARIFIED AND ADDRESSED:

1. QUALIFICATION PROCESS OF THE SALES TEAM

2. SELLING AT THE RIGHT LEVEL

3. CONTROL OF THE SALES CYCLE

Inaccurate forecasting can almost always be traced back to at least one of these three issues. The result not only reflects poorly on the senior sales executive, sales managers, and the sales team, but it is extremely costly to the company. In our survey of hundreds of sales executives and company presidents, we asked the question: "What percentage of your sales pursuits ends up in a 'No Decision' or a loss?"

A sales pursuit for this survey was defined as any perceived opportunity that a salesperson spends resources on. The answers may be surprising to some, but not when you understand the severity of the problem. The answers have ranged from 35% to a high of 90%! Bad sales pursuits cost an organization in opportunity, time, travel, and expense.

As an example, let's explore the costly effect to an organization that has a sales force of 50 sellers with a quota of $1,000,000 equaling total revenues of $50,000,000. If this team beats the norm and only gets involved in bad sales pursuits 20% of the time, the impact on the revenue is $10,000,000 annually.

The Summit group is a research firm that shows that the average sales person costs about $300 per hour. They go further to tell us the average preparation and travel time for a face-to-face sales call is 10 hours. If we assume the normal face-to-face business call is approximately 1 hour this all adds up to $3,300 per sales call. Think how much it is really costing if your averages sales pursuit ends up in a "no decision."

Just as important, as salespeople change their approach, their organizations must have a shift in mindset as well. The idea that an organization can build a superior product with the latest technology, service or solution, and that it will basically sell itself has always been a flawed thought process. In today's competitive world of business, this idea is not a successful way to think or run an organization.

Too many organizations today take the approach of hiring sales people, putting them through a company orientation process and then turn them lose to sink or swim. The orientation is typically an overview of the organization and generalized training on the product and/or services the organization offers. What needs to change is teaching the sales people about the market trend, the decision makers' roles, the current issues, others affected by these issues in the organization, a complete understanding of the terms they need to know, and then teaching them how their company's offerings address the issues of the executives at both a personal and business level.

When do senior executives get involved in major purchase decisions?
Recent studies show that executives are more involved during the beginning and end of the buying process, and less involved in the middle.

At the beginning of the buying process, executives get involved in order to:
• Understand current business issues
• Establish objectives
• Set the overall strategy

Executives get involved at the end of the buying process in order to:
• Plan the implementation of the new purchase

• Measure the results of the decision

How can salespeople gain access to decision makers?

The eight most common reasons for granting a meeting to a salesperson are:

1. The ability of the salesperson to understand their issues
2. A recommendation from a credible source inside the executive's organization
3. An existing relationship with the seller
4. The reputation of the salesperson's company
5. A need for the product or service the salesperson is offering
6. An external referral from the respected source
7. The timing of the salesperson's request for the meeting (as related to the buying cycle)
8. Being able to relate to the executive's issues

How do executives test salespeople?

Most executives give salespeople only five minutes to establish some kind of relationship. Within those five minutes, salespeople should:

Speak from a business prospective, demonstrating the homework they've done to develop an understanding of the prospect's key issues.

Raise relevant questions and share new business perspectives.

Listen and understand rather than attempting to sell their product or service during the first contact with an executive. "Get the answers to the test."

Executives are most likely to grant meetings with salespeople who:

Understand the prospect's key business drivers and business initiatives.

Convey how they can deliver value to the executive's company.

Do not turn on the executive's "Sales Security System."

Be confident, professional, flexible, and honest because this is what the executive expects.

What does the executive desire prior to meeting with salespeople?

Executives rank first those salespeople who understand the customer's key business goals and objectives.

Executives want salespeople who will listen and consider the customer's needs before proposing a solution.

Executives want salespeople who understand industry trends, common terms, and the issues they face everyday.

How can salespeople establish credibility with executives?

Executives rank salespeople's ability to marshal resources from within their organization as also very important.

Executives rank salespeople's willingness to be held accountable as most important.

Executives state they want salespeople who understand their goals and objectives, and who are responsive to their requests. They rate a salesperson that disparages the competition as least credible.

Above all, executives value decisive and confident salespeople. They do not value arrogance and "hard sell" approaches.

When is "trusted advisor" selling necessary?

Sixty-eight percent of executives think "executive-to-executive" selling is of significant importance, mainly to reaffirm the seller's commitment and highlight the strategic fit for their companies.

The Fundamentals of Salesmanship

Whether you have been in sales for years or are just starting out, try evaluating your current knowledge in the Quid Pro Quo selling areas listed below. Be honest.

For more information about these specific areas, take a Quid Pro Quo training course. For more information, see www.salesbuilders.com.

How well do you do the following? (One being least.)

1. Use consultative Quid Pro Quo selling techniques? 1 2 3 4

2. Build and use customer referrals? Do you have a network helping you find prospects? 1 2 3 4

3. Develop more effective questioning techniques? Sometimes it is not what you ask but how you ask it. 1 2 3 4

4. Shorten the sales cycle? Do you control the time frame for each step of the sales cycle? 1 2 3 4

5. Understand what it takes to be successful? Learn how to be your own sales manager or boss. 1 2 3 4

6. Personalize each sale? Sell at the personal level. 1 2 3 4

7. Reduce perceived risk of committing? Make it easy for prospects to say, "Yes." 1 2 3 4

8. Use the entire qualification process? The secret of qualification is how you ask, not what you ask. 1 2 3 4

9. Maximize your current customer base? Strategize how to get more out of your customers. 1 2 3 4

10. Understand buying motives? Why do prospects buy? 1 2 3 4

11. Run your own franchise? Create ways to succeed. 1 2 3 4

12. Make use of consultative sales strategy? You may win or lose sales, but you may not always know why. 1 2 3 4

13. Establish sales goals? Do you establish clear objectives for yourself in sales? 1 2 3 4

14. Define your target market? Identify a qualified prospect. 1 2 3 4

15. Use basic sales skills? In all aspects of sales. 1 2 3 4

16. Report sales? Understanding how sales are measured. 1 2 3 4

17. Do you use true presentation skills or just transfer knowledge? 1 2 3 4

18. Develop a larger sales pipeline? Learn new prospecting techniques. 1 2 3 4

19. Increase market awareness on your own? Telemarketing, direct mail, dinner programs. 1 2 3 4

20. Understand the sales cycle? Put yourself in the prospect's shoes. 1 2 3 4

21. How well do you not accept a negative response but instead turn a "No" into "Yes"? 1 2 3 4

22. Convince prospects that they have issues you can solve? Have prospects buy willingly versus feeling you're selling them. 1 2 3 4

23. Follow a structured, consistent sales approach? Know exactly where you are in the sales cycle. 1 2 3 4

24. Prevent premature elaboration? Sell before you have all the facts. 1 2 3 4

25. Understand the two organizations every company has? Who holds the power? 1 2 3 4

26. Forecast when your agreements will be signed. Manage the pipeline. 1 2 3 4

What's Your Grade? Add up your total.

93 to 100 = A, Congratulations!

84 to 92 = B, Okay.

73 to 84 = C, You are as close to the bottom as to the top.

Below 73 = Visit www.salesbuilders.com

Listening Skills

Too many representatives lose great opportunities by forgetting the very simple formula that follows:

Formula for Handling People
By General George C. Marshall

SOLDIER, STATESMEN, AND NOBLE PRIZE WINNER

1. LISTEN TO THE OTHER PERSON'S STORY.

2. LISTEN TO THE OTHER PERSON'S FULL STORY.

3. LISTEN TO THE OTHER PERSON'S FULL STORY WITH YOUR HEART.

....

THE LISTENING LADDER

THE SIX STEPS TO BECOMING A BETTER LISTENER FORM A LADDER.

....

L LOOK AT THE PERSON SPEAKING TO YOU.

A ASK QUESTIONS.

D DON'T INTERRUPT.

D DON'T CHANGE THE SUBJECT.

E EMPATHIZE.

R RESPOND VERBALLY AND NON-VERBALLY.

If you are sincere and understand the value of trying to help people solve problems, and if you truly want to understand the other person, your selling will take on a life of it own and become second nature for you.

Ten Steps to Sales Success

The list below contains ten actions that will make a difference in your sales success. Copy the list. Hang it by your phone. Leave copies where you'll see them often. Carry out these actions. Your sales manager will thank you. And your checkbook will thank you, too.

1. Establish a give-and-take (Quid Pro Quo) relationship.

By now, you should be very familiar with how a give-and-take relationship applies in selling.

2. Sell. Don't tell.

When giving a demonstration, be sure you're not giving a class on how to use your product. I like to follow this rule: 80% of the time you need to be establishing rapport, qualifying, and positioning yourself for the close, and the other 20% of the time you should be proving that your product will meet the prospect's needs. Sales representatives who don't follow a structured sales methodology typically have these percentages reversed. Stay on track and in control by demonstrating only what the prospect needs to see in order to convince him to buy your product. Like I said, you're not giving a "how to" class on everything your product can do.

3. Stress features, benefits and differences.

If you've ever had any sales training, the first topic covered should have been features/benefits statements. These statements simply point out a feature of your product, service, or company, and explain the benefit of the feature as it relates to the prospect's personal or business situation. Your next step in the process is to point out those factors which differentiate your features and benefits from those of any competitor.

Never assume you're the only person the prospect is talking to. Most prospective buyers are in one of two situations. Either they are handling the problem you are trying to solve for them in some unproductive way or there is a competitor pitching another solution to their issues.

Since either or both of these may be the case, you absolutely need to differentiate your features and benefits from the alternatives available. It's important not to disparage a competitor or any other alternative. Simply point out the differences and explain why, based on all the information you've gotten from the prospect, your solution is different and better.

4. Act. Don't react.

One of the keys of Quid Pro Quo selling is staying in control of the prospect throughout the sales cycle. The idea is to act, not react. From time to time, a prospect will try to push your buttons. Sometimes, he is trying to test your conviction and product knowledge; other times he's just trying to get a reaction out of you. Always act in a way that shows you are prepared and professional, and you'll earn credibility with your prospect.

5. Ask open-ended questions.

If you're having trouble getting your prospects to open up and talk with you, then you're not asking enough good, open-ended questions. The chapter on qualification contains many examples of open-ended questions. Write down these questions and keep them close. Never give your prospect the opportunity to answer "yes" or "no."

6. Keep "so what?" In mind.

Every time I address a group. I picture "So what?" written across everyone's forehead. Even now as I write this book, I imagine "So what?" written on every reader's forehead. The point is, prospects are always asking, "So what?" They want to know what your product or service will do for them. Why should they care if it's got, for example, a self-programming feature?

What does that mean for them? Why should they care about any of the features of your product?

When pitching their companies, many representatives often say something like, "ABC is the fastest-growing company in our industry." It may sound impressive, but your prospect is probably thinking, "So what?" You've got to point out why this fact is important.

Try this, "ABC is the fastest-growing company in our industry, which means that you have the security of knowing our product works and our customers are happy. If this weren't true, we'd be out of business instead of being the fasting-growing company in our market." Remember, when selling, assume the prospect knows nothing. It's always better to over-explain than have a prospect miss an important point.

7. Be enthusiastic.

Here's another pretty simple concept that many representatives overlook. You've got to be enthusiastic about what you're selling. Keep a mirror on your desk so you can look at your face occasionally while you're on the phone. If you don't look happy and enthusiastic, you probably don't sound it either. On face-to-face sales calls, be excited to be there. The person you are talking to is going to pay for your child's next year in college or help you buy that beach house you have always wanted! If you keep that in mind, it'll be easy to be enthusiastic.

8. Be interested.

It's one thing to act interested; it's something entirely different to be interested. Even if you are in a business-to-business market place, you need to sell at the personal level. Get to know your prospects. Bond with them. Find out how business issues affect them on a personal level. Be genuinely interested in helping your prospects resolve their issues. As you help your prospects solve their problems, you create lasting rapport. Not only have you sold your product, but in many cases, you will have made a friend.

9. Ask for referrals.

The best way to get referrals is to ask for them. Personally, I'd ask for a referral after every single call, regardless of whether or not the prospect bought. It's human nature to want to help other people in need. If you've given a good-natured, professional sales pitch, and the prospect just keeps saying, "No," ask him to help you and refer someone who might have an interest.

On one occasion, a prospect who never bought anything from me gave me twelve good referrals! Don't make the mistake of waiting until the prospect buys your product and is using it successfully before you ask for a referral. Ask after every call. Everyone knows someone, and that someone needs to know you!

10. Cement the sale.

Cementing the sale is done by reviewing with the prospect all the reasons they are buying your product. Remember to stress benefits and to differentiate your product from the competition. Cementing the sale reminds prospects of their problems and how your product is going to serve their needs. By cementing every sale, you'll be going a long way to eliminate buyer's remorse, which affects most buyers.

Checklist for Closing the Sale

If you follow the charted course for sales success and execute each step effectively, closing the sale will be the easiest part of the sales cycle. An important step is for you to learn how to "read" the prospect along the way. By accurately reading the prospect's attitude, you'll know when to stop selling and start closing. I've always found using a checklist to track my progress through the sales process is a big help, especially when I'm working with multiple prospects simultaneously.

A Few Tips

If you think you are losing a deal, even a little bit, you are! If you are not hearing a little "Yes" all along the way, be prepared for one big "No" at the end.

Even though you think you're in control, it's important to constantly evaluate your progress. If you feel you're getting stonewalled at any point along the way, there's a good chance you haven't uncovered the real issues.

Qualified prospects will tell you what they are thinking, where you stand, and what their current positions are. Obviously the better-qualified your prospect, the better chances. Always continue selling prospects who are on the fence. Never accept "No!"

Points to Check When Closing a Sale

Are you dealing with the decision maker?

Do the prospects need/desire your product?

Are the funds to pay available?

Have you done a presentation?

Are there any outstanding issues?

Do you understand their buying motives?

Have you addressed every objection?

Do they know the benefits of your product?

Do the prospects have a sense of urgency?

Have you created a sense of urgency?

Have they given you referrals?

Have you done everything possible to close?

You should constantly review this checklist and you should always have a good feel for where you stand.

Closing Questions to Ask Yourself
1. What needs can you meet?
2. Can you clearly articulate your prospect's needs? More importantly, has the prospect articulated them to you?
3. Why would your prospect spend money for your solution at this time? Why didn't he solve this problem six months ago? What happens if he doesn't act and has the same issues six months from now?
4. When does the prospect plan to change his habits? Why and how? Why is he buying OR NOT buying? What are the alternatives?

LEARN THE SECRETS OF THE QUID PRO QUO SELLING APPROACH FROM BOB BECK

Whether you are a one-person salesforce or manage a salesforce of 25,000 you can learn Bob Beck's unique approach. Cities include:

Atlanta	New York
Los Angles	San Francisco
Tampa	Houston
Dallas	London
Chicago	Boston

To learn more on attending a Quid Pro Quo course in your area or to bring Bob Beck to your company call Sales Builders Inc., today.

THE "QUID PRO QUO" SERIES

Results focused sales approach, teaches your sales team how to control the sales cycle with a true consultative sales approach while employing an authentic franchise mentality.

The course is tailord to help you close real-life situations, find new business, and enable you to see whole new opportunities. There is no faster way to realize results from the Quid Pro Quo approach than to apply the techniques to your current opportunites.

SELLING LIKE YOU OWN THE FRANCHISE

Teaches your sales team how to create and find new sales opportunities without corporate marketing. A sales territory is a sales person's franchise and this course teaches them how to run it successfully. This course will eliminate the excuse: "I can't succeed because I don't get enough leads."

Ninety-three precent of sales people have not been formally trained how to build a pipeline of prospects. Your sales team will sell to the right level after taking the Quid Pro Quo course.

QUID PRO QUO FOR PROJECT MANAGERS

Everyone needs to sell! Project managers & account managers are your company's "trojan horses." They are typically not trained to sell and usually do not want to be perceived as sales people.

We integrate Quid Pro Quo with their day-to-day customer issues, teach them to identify new revenue opportunities, extend their engagements, control client's expectations and improve relationships with clients.

NEW FROM SALESBUILDERS: EXECUTIVE LINK

Executive Link is the first and only tool that links your sales team to executive roles. Executive Link will detail the issues they face, the others that are effected by these issues, why the issues exist, industry trends, industry terms, and solutions.

We even give you the ability to customize the solutions to your products or services in manufacturing, logistics, healthcare, financial services, banking, insurance, telecommunications, retail, distributors, and the public sector. With the Quid Pro Quo selling approach your sales team will more effectively be able to:

- project themselves into the executives' shoes
- know the issues that keep the executives awake at night
- be able to "talk the talk"
- achieve the status of "trusted advisor"

HOW TO START

CALL: 770.497.8572 OR 404.822.9082
EMAIL: SALES@SALESBUILDERS.COM
WEB: WWW.SALESBUILDERS.COM